MALING

The Trademark of Excellence

By

Steven Moore

and

Catherine Ross

Authors' Acknowledgements

The Authors would like to thank the many people who have helped to make this book possible. The task of researching the pottery's history was made easier and pleasanter by the invaluable help given by members of the Maling and Hoult families and many of the pottery's former employees. Particular thanks is due to: Mr and Mrs L.G. Boullemier, Mr Cecil Parker, Mrs V.T. Griffin, Mr F.W. Hoult, Mr R. Allen, Mr J. Allen, Miss N. Allen, Miss P. Longley, Mr T. Boullemier, Mr and Mrs Waggett, Mr F.J. Dennett, Mrs Fordham, Mrs Rhodes, Miss Tromans. We would also like to acknowledge the help and encouragement given by the following: Mrs Arnott, Mrs V. Proudfoot, Mr and Mrs P. Moore, Mr G. Corran, Ian Sharp, Tony Henderson, Mrs N. Varty, Erica Gorman and Mr N.L. Heslop.

We are particularly pleased at the quantity of illustrations that the book contains and we are grateful to all the Maling collectors and owners who allowed their pieces to be photographed; owner's credits are included in the captions to the photographs. We would also like to thank the copyright holders of the archive material, particularly Tableware International for allowing us to reproduce material from *The Pottery Gazette*. The quantity of photographs in the book has been made possible by the sponsorship of Ringtons Ltd., and Anderson & Garland, both of whom generously helped meet some of the production costs. The photographs were taken by Les Golding and we would like to thank both him and the book's designer, Vicki Taylor, for the hard and excellent work that they have put in.

Abbreviations used in the photograph captions

AB	Mr A. Bainbridge
DB	Mr D. Boardman
F	Fenwicks Ltd
FH	Mr F. W. Hoult
GW	Mr and Mrs G. White
KW	Mr and Mrs K. Watson
LAG	Laing Art Gallery, Newcastle (Tyne and Wear Museums Service)
PC	Private Collection
SAG	Shipley Art Gallery, Gateshead (Tyne and Wear Museums Service)
SM	Steven Moore

Other Abbreviations used in the text

M	Mark (see appendix 1)
MTP	*Maling, a Tyneside Pottery*, R.C. Bell, S. Cottle, and L. Dixon (Tyne and Wear County Council Museums, 1981)
pn	Pattern number
TP	*Tyneside Pottery*, R.C. Bell, (Studio Vista, 1971)

In the photograph captions pattern names in inverted commas are marked on the piece itself.

ISBN 0 905974 46 8
© Tyne and Wear Museums Service, 1989
Published by Tyne and Wear Museums Service, Blandford House, Blandford Square, Newcastle upon Tyne

Photography: Les Golding, Tyne and Wear Museums Service
Design: Vicki Taylor, Newcastle City Council Graphics Department
Typeset by True North, Newcastle upon Tyne
Printed by E.F. Peterson and Son, South Shields

Front cover: Detail of Tulip pattern plate, c.1932
Back cover: Seagull vase modelled by Norman Carling, c.1944

Foreword

Maling pottery must be one of Tyneside's best ambassadors. The stylish and colourful pottery produced in Newcastle by C.T. Maling & Sons is now eagerly collected by people all over the world and from all walks of life. Tyne and Wear Museums Service is delighted to be able to foster the already strong interest taken in Maling pottery by the publication of this new book.

When the kilns of Maling's Ford Pottery in Byker were finally extinguished in 1963, it brought to an end one of the most remarkable stories of success in the modern pottery industry. With a history stretching back to 1762, the firm was one of the oldest pottery manufacturers in the country. It was also, in its heyday, one of the largest and certainly one of the most versatile: Maling's produced everything from ordinary jam jars to high quality tableware. Maling's was a pottery that the North East could be proud of.

'Maling: The Trademark of Excellence' is the successor to 'Maling, a Tyneside Pottery' published by Tyne and Wear Museums Service in 1981 and reprinted in 1984. Building on the success of the former book, this new publication adds a considerable amount of new research to the story of the pottery, together with a mass of indispensible practical information for the collector. The book is the joint work of Dr. Catherine Ross of Tyne and Wear Museums Service, and Mr. Steven Moore, whose enthusiasm for Maling pottery is more than evident in the many splendid pieces from his collection illustrated in the following pages. The Museums Service is grateful to Mr Moore, and to the other members of the public who have contributed to the book in various ways. The help received from the public in the writing of this book is a measure of the affection which still surrounds the name of Maling here on Tyneside.

We would also like to thank Ringtons Ltd. and Anderson & Garland, who both helped to meet some of the book's production costs. Without their help, the number of illustrations in the book would have been reduced.

We feel sure that this book will be warmly received by collectors and non-collectors alike. We are also confident that the story it tells will enrich both the understanding and the appreciation of the industrial and artistic heritage of the North East, an aim which is central to the work of Tyne and Wear Museums Service.

Councillor Barney Rice, J.P.
Chairman, Tyne and Wear Museums Joint Committee

John Thompson
Director, Tyne and Wear Museums Service

Contents

1.1

Chapter 1

The history of C.T. Maling & Sons

C.T. Maling & Sons was Tyneside's largest, best known and longest lived firm of pottery manufacturers. When the firm closed in 1963 it was the end of a 201 year life that had begun at Sunderland in 1762 and had grown to maturity on Tyneside during the 19th century. In its heyday the company employed over 1,000 people, and could boast of having the largest pottery site in Great Britain, possibly the world. The story of Maling's is a story of pottery success, all the more remarkable for being the story of an 'out pottery', far from the heart of the British pottery industry in Staffordshire. This success was partly due to the enterprise of the Maling family themselves but it is also a tribute to the skills and loyalty of their Tyneside workforce which included many families who, like the Malings, had connections with the firm stretching back over several generations.

The North Hylton Pottery

The first Maling pottery was established at North Hylton near Sunderland in 1762 by William Maling of Sunderland (1698-1765). By the 1760s the Malings had been living in England for 200 years but the family was originally French, and the Sunderland Malings claimed to be able to trace their ancestry back to one Guillame de St. Malin, a bodyguard of Charles III of France. The family were Huguenots and in 1562 another Guillame Maling had fled the religious persecution in his own country to settle in Filey on the Yorkshire coast. The Malings became merchants and prospered.

William Maling of Sunderland had inherited wealth from this side of the family but his fortune had been considerably enhanced by his marriage in 1740 to Catherine Thompson of Hendon, the daughter of a wealthy landowner. By the time that the pottery was founded in 1762 William was a well established figure in Sunderland with profitable interests in coal, shipping and timber. Pottery manufacturing would have been a sensible complement to these existing business interests: William Maling's ships could set sail from Sunderland laden with pottery that had been fired with coal from his collieries; the ships could then return from Scandinavian ports laden with timber for use in his timber yard.

William Maling died in 1765 and his fortune and business interests passed to his two sons, Christopher Thompson (1741-1810), and John (1746-1823) (fig. 1.1). The eldest son seems to have distanced himself from the family's commercial interests by pursuing a career in Government service. During the 1780s he was living in France, where he married his second wife Maria Sophia, but by 1790 he had returned to the North East of England. This branch of the Malings did very well for themselves thanks to the marriage of C.T. Maling's second daughter, Sophia, to Lord Mulgrave, the First Lord of the Admiralty. Mulgrave was an unashamed practitioner of nepotism and thanks to him every member of his wife's family was given government sinecures. C.T. Maling himself ended up as the Commissioner of Excise.

John Maling appears to have played a more active part in the commercial life

1.1 John Maling of the North Hylton Pottery (1746-1823).

OUSEBURN BRIDGE POTTERY.

RULES
AND
REGULATIONS

TO BE OBSERVED BY
Persons employed at the above Pottery.

No Ale, Beer, or Spirit to be brought to, or drank within the Manufactory, except the stated allowance for the Firemen—Fine Two Shillings and Sixpence.

Any Person going into any other Workshop than his own, without leave being asked and obtained, either at meal times or any other time, will be fined One Shilling, or if after the regular work hours, Two Shillings and Sixpence.

Persons employed not to bring their own, or permit other Children to come to the Manufactory, except such as are actually working there, or bringing in Meals, in which case they must immediately leave—Fine One Shilling.

The Workshops to be kept clean by the Person or Persons employed therein, if neglected—Fine One Shilling.

Turners and others to permit no Iron Filings or other Dirt to be mixed among the Clay, Shavings or Broken Ware—Fine One Shilling.

Persons using Moulds not to permit the same to remain in the Stoves, except when in use—Fine Two Shillings and Sixpence.

Gaming and Amusements of every description are forbid within the Manufactory—Fine Two Shillings and Sixpence.

All Workshop Doors to be locked at Six o'Clock, any Work then on Moulds will be destroyed.

Any Person leaving Boards, Shovels, Baskets, or any Utensils in the Yard, will be Fined One Shilling.

No Strangers to be admitted into the Manufactory without leave from the Office, or the Person whom he comes to see will be Fined One Shilling.

No Dogs allowed to come into the Yard—Fine One Shilling.

All Pressed Ware to be stuck together the same Day as made, and finished off first thing next morning, if not it will be broken, and the offending Person Fined One Shilling.

All Copperplates to be cleaned immediately after being used—Fine One Shilling.

Any Person Swearing, found Drunk, Fighting, or *any disorderly behaviour*—Fine Two Shillings and Sixpence.

Any Person using Round Coals on any Stove or Fire—Fine One Shilling.

Any Person throwing Stones or Clay about either Yard or Workshops—Fine Sixpence.

All Shavings and Broken Ware to be carried out at Six o'Clock each morning in Summer, or Day-break in Winter—Fine Sixpence.

Any Person leaving his or her employment, without giving due notice, will forfeit the wages due to them.

Any person not doing work in the manner ordered, will be held responsible for any damage or loss that may arise from his not attending to instructions.

Any Workshop wherein these Rules shall be found damaged or destroyed, the Person or Persons employed therein shall be fined Five Shillings.

All Persons engaging themselves to work will be considered as having agreed to work under these Rules and Regulations.

1.2

1.4

of the North East, notably by becoming a partner in the first Sunderland bank, Russell, Allen, Maling & Wade. Banking was a profitable business and in 1784 he was able to build himself a new house, The Grange at Bishopwearmouth. Although John Maling is said to have ridden over to the pottery at North Hylton daily to oversee matters, agents were employed to manage the concern. A notice in the *Newcastle Courant* of 1790 names John Dawson of Hylton and W. Lees of Sunderland as the pottery's agents entitled to receive money on behalf of the proprietors, Christopher and John Maling.

The Ouseburn Bridge Pottery

The death of Christopher Maling in 1810 appears to have put the pottery more completely into the hands of John Maling. By this time the older man had been joined in the business by his sons John and Robert (1781-1863), and it was said to have been Robert (fig. 1.2) rather than his 78 year old father who was responsible for the transfer of the pottery from Wearside to Tyneside. Although the move was a continuation of the old business at North Hylton, it was also a new venture in that a completely new pottery was erected at the Ouseburn Bridge to the east of Newcastle where a little colony of manufacturing concerns already existed. According to an old kiln book preserved at the pottery, the first kiln at the Ouseburn Bridge was fired on June 28, 1817.

The attractions of Tyneside for an early nineteenth century pottery manufacturer such as Robert Maling were summed up by the writer Eneas Mackenzie in his *History of Northumberland* of 1825:

> The banks of the Tyne offer many facilities for manufacturing every species of earthenware. Flint and potter's clay are brought from the south of England in ships coming in ballast for coals; glass is plentiful here; and the chief materials for colouring and glazing are productions of the neighbourhood. Yet all these advantages were long overlooked or neglected; and till of late years large importations of earthenware annually entered the Tyne. Our manufacturers are rapidly increasing in skill and dexterity and in their productions almost equal that of Staffordshire.

In Robert Maling's case a further attraction of the Tyne was undoubtedly the extensive shipping trade carried on from the river. One of the few pieces of information we have about Robert Maling is that he was 'manufacturing chiefly for the Dutch market'.

The move to Tyneside was undoubtedly a successful one. The pottery prospered, and by the 1840s Robert Maling's brother John had taken over a second pottery, the Old Ouseburn Pottery, which he occupied until 1864. By the time of Robert's death in 1863 the management of the Ouseburn Bridge Pottery was in the hands of his second son, Christopher Thompson Maling (1824-1901) and it was to be this third generation Maling who was to have the most profound effect on the pottery's development.

C.T. Maling and the Ford A Pottery

Christopher Thompson Maling (fig. 1.4) was an archetypal entrepreneur, ambitious and ever eager to keep his firm ahead of his competitors. Under his direction the Maling pottery interest was transformed almost beyond recognition. In 1853 he took over a small pottery producing a modest range of conventional earthenware. On his death in 1901 he left what was claimed to be the biggest earthenware factory in the world.

The root of C.T. Maling's success lay in his conviction that his pottery should concentrate not on run of the mill domestic tableware but on wholesale commercial pottery such as jam jars and preserve pots. This conviction is said to have taken root during the time he spent as a young man working as a traveller for his father's firm. Whilst on a trip to Scotland he is said to have struck up a friendship with the redoubtable Keiller sisters of Dundee, already well established as makers of jams and marmalades. The sisters placed an order for a crate of earthenware jars, followed by another, and then another until C.T. Maling found that jam jars were taking up more and more of his order book. The custom of the Keillers was to provide a solid source of income for Maling's until the 1930s.

C.T. Maling also believed that the key to success in the pottery industry lay in

1.3

1.2 Robert Maling of the Ouseburn Bridge Pottery (1781-1863).
1.3 Christopher Thompson Maling (1824-1901).
1.4 Rules of the Ouseburn Bridge Pottery, mid 19th century (LAG).

mechanisation, and in 1859 he had the opportunity to put this belief into practice when he erected a new, larger pottery at the Ouseburn. This was the first Ford Pottery, named after Mary Ford, the daughter of an Edinburgh glass manufacturer, whom C.T. had married in 1857; it was said to be her generous dowry that enabled the Ford Pottery to be built on such an ambitious scale (fig. 1.5). The Ford Pottery dwarfed its predecessor at the Ouseburn Bridge. The new factory was said to produce more pots in a week than the old pottery had produced in a year and this astonishing increase was partly explained by the fact that some of the production processes at the Ford Pottery had been adapted to steam machinery. C.T. Maling's evidence to the Children's Employment Commission of 1863 makes his interest in machines quite clear:

> We make cups, bowls, mugs, jars, jugs and tea pots by machinery; we employ women and girls to make them at wages varying from 3s to 4s 6d per week ..... The ware we principally make by machinery are jelly cans or jars. I believe oval ware and dishes might be made by machinery if a great number of particular shapes was required. Many kinds of fancy ware such as jugs and tureens etc. could not be made by machinery as they would require finishing afterwards.

The success of Maling's new pottery was summed up in 1878 by Llewellyn Jewitt in *The Ceramic Art of Great Britain*. His account is also interesting for stating the advantages that Maling's machine made pots enjoyed over their hand potted competitors:

> The works (the Ford Pottery) were erected for the purpose of manufacturing by machinery the various goods produced by Mr Maling, the main bulk of which are marmalade, jam and extract of beef pots. These are of a very fine and compact white body, with an excellent glaze made from borax without any lead; and it is said that at least 95% of the pots used by wholesale manufacturers in Great Britain are made at this establishment. The pots being entirely made by machinery are necessarily much more uniform in size and weight and thickness than those produced by any other process, and these, as well as the excellence of body and glaze, are advantages which have been appreciated.

1.5

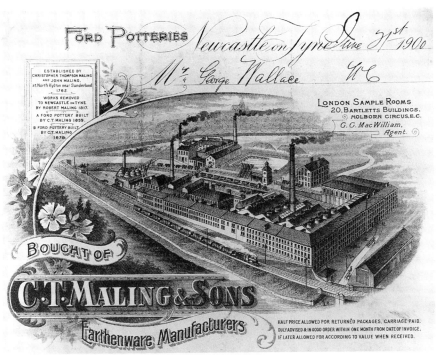

1.6

The Ford B Pottery

By the time that this account of the Ford Pottery was published C.T. Maling was moving on to even bigger scales of production. New markets, new production techniques and new methods of transport had opened up new opportunities and in characteristically ambitious style C.T. Maling decided to meet these new opportunities by investing £100,000 in the erection of yet another new pottery. The new pottery was the massive Ford B Pottery which was begun in 1878 on a 14 acre site half a mile to the east of the old Ford Pottery, now renamed the Ford A Pottery. In the same way that the Ford A Pottery had dwarfed its predecessor, so the Ford B Pottery introduced manufacturing on an unprecedentedly large scale. The new pottery could produce more in a month than the old one had done in a year; it had ten kilns and the production process was as mechanised as it could be; over 1,000 hands were employed and the whole staggering enterprise was indeed, as the Malings claimed, the largest pottery in Great Britain, possibly the world (figs. 1.6 – 1.13).

One explanation for the massive size of the Ford B Pottery was that it really was several different factories all under one roof. The pottery included all the subsidiary operations that a pottery relied on, from grinding and preparing the raw flints, to engraving the copper plates used for transfer printing. In Staffordshire these operations were usually carried out by small specialist firms, but the Ford B Pottery was an 'out pottery' and self-sufficiency was to some extent forced upon it. The pottery was laid out so that each stage of the manufacturing process followed on from the other with the minimum delay. The process began at the flint mill where the massive 500 horse power engine ground 400 tons of flint stones to powder every week. The flint mill was also claimed to be the largest in the country and although most of the ground flint was used at the Ford potteries some was sold commercially to other potteries in the North East and Scotland.

The manufacturing process would continue through the pottery workshops where the vessels would be formed by mechanised or semi-mechanised means, fired in biscuit kilns, dipped, glazed, decorated or finished, fired in glost kilns until

1.5 The Ford A Pottery opened in 1859.
1.6 View of the Ford B Pottery shown on C.T. Maling & Sons' bill head (SM).

6

eventually the finished goods would end up packed in straw in crates which were either taken to the steamers at St. Peter's Quay or loaded onto the trucks standing on the ¾ mile of railway sidings that lay within the pottery walls. A description of the pottery in 1894 stated that on some days eighteen trucks, each containing nearly 1,000 dozen pieces, would be dispatched by rail from the pottery.

Altogether the Ford B Pottery was a remarkable example of self sufficiency and even 38 years after its opening it was still exciting admiration in the industry:

> Rarely have I seen in an English pottery evidence of work proceed more automatically or economically. Right from the sliphouse to the finished warehouse the arrangements dovetail into one another in a manner remindful of the parts of a big machine. In every way the factory is self contained, and particularly noticeable in this respect is an extensive mill for grinding and preparation of raw materials which enables the firm not only to fulfil all their own requirements in this respect but

1.7 2 photographs of the Ford B Pottery from the north, taken in 1898 by F.T. Maling (PC). Some of the buildings are named in the original print, other identifications have been added where known. 1. The 'Ivory Clay Sliphouse, Designer's studio, Electroplating shop, die stamping, engineering shop'; the engraving, decorating and gilding shops are further to the left. 2. The flint drying pans where the water would be driven off the liquid mixture which emerged from the flint mill. 3. The bridge carrying an open trough of liquid flint from the flint mill to the flint drying pans. 4. The cottage which was on the site when the Malings bought it in 1878 and which was used as a stable and harness store.

1.7

actually to supply other potters with milled materials, a remarkable achievement for an out pottery, surely.

(*The Pottery Gazette*, 1916)

The new pottery was undoubtedly up to date in its efficient layout, but it also provided relatively advanced conditions for the women and men who spent their working lives inside it. The Ford B Pottery did its best to avoid the hazards of breathing in air laden with clay dust and poisonous lead fumes by providing well ventilated and light workshops, and also making use of leadless glazes. Good working conditions were said to be one of the reasons why the pottery succeeded in attracting skilled workers from Staffordshire. Even as late as the 1930s the spacious rooms of the Ford B Pottery were still infinitely preferable to the cramped conditions that obtained in many Staffordshire factories.

C.T. Maling was said to have been a good employer and by the time that the Ford B Pottery opened, he had already established a chapel and school for the benefit of his employees (figs. 1.14 and 1.15). The Ford B Pottery was designed to

5. The lithograph shop, modelling shop, mould and block store (the valuable moulds were stored well away from the kilns to minimise the risk of fire damage). 6. 'Clock tower and Fire Brigade Station'. 7. The pottery's main entrance front containing the offices, showroom and glost warehouses. 8. The main making departments containing the biscuit and glost kilns, casting shops, dipping houses and jollying shops. 9. Hoffman kilns used to fire the saggars. 10. Saggar making and mould making departments, plaster of paris store. 11. The Boiler house containing the steam engine. The flint mill is further to the right.

1.8

1.9

1.8 Photograph of the Ford B Pottery from its east side, taken by F.T. Maling in 1898 (PC). This view shows the reservoirs which supplied water to the steam engine and the flint mill.

1.9 'The Dipping house', photograph taken by F.T. Maling in 1898 (PC).

1.10 'The Large Jolly Shop', where hollow items were made using a 'jolly' or revolving mould, and the 'plate makers department'; photograph taken by F.T. Maling in 1898 (PC).

1.11 'Two of the largest pots we have jollied up to 1890, 3 ft. high, 2 ft. diam. Held 60 gallons of water'; photograph taken by F.T. Maling in 1898 (PC).

1.12 The main steam engine at the Ford B Pottery, a 500 hp. Corliss Valve engine which was replaced by an electric generator in 1925; photograph taken by F.T. Maling in 1898 (PC).

1.13 Maling's junction on the North Eastern Railway showing the lines going right into the middle of the pottery. The flint mill is the massive building on the far right; the building with twin chimneys is the boiler house. Photograph taken by F.T. Maling in 1898 (PC).

1.14 Bookplate from the Ford Pottery School, 1889 (SM).

1.15 Sampler sewn at the Ford Pottery School, 1896 (PC).

1.10

include adequate washrooms, dining rooms and kitchens where the workers could cook their own meals, and the spare land outside the boundary wall was divided up into allotments for the employees. C.T. Malings's policy here was not entirely disinterested for he is said to have looked on the allotments as an additional 'security perimeter' for the pottery. By the 1890s the workforce numbered over 1,000 a large proportion of whom would have been women.

1.12

1.11

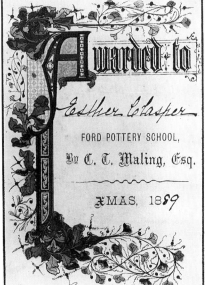

1.14

1.15

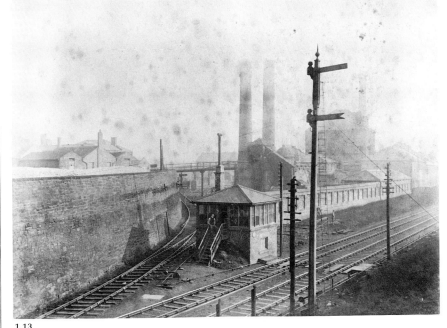

1.13

New decorative wares

The building of the Ford B Pottery was the catalyst that persuaded the firm to branch out into new types of earthenware production. The new pottery 'could produce more jam pots than there was demand for' so new ranges were introduced to use up the extra manufacturing capacity. The range of wholesale wares was greatly extended to include such things as sanitary ware, photographic and chemical apparatus, water filters, electrical ware, kitchen and dairy equipment. More importantly, the firm embarked on the production of fashionably decorated toilet and table ware. The impetus behind this is said to have come from C.T. Maling's three sons, John Ford (1858-1924), Christopher Thompson (1863-1934), and Frederick Theodore (1866-1937), all of whom were brought into the business during the 1880s to create, in 1889, the firm of C.T. Maling & Sons. The older man still favoured commercial ware and is said to have wanted the firm to expand by going into the production of glass jam jars.

The production of decorated pottery probably began in 1883 and it was certainly well under way by 1885 when C.T. Maling registered his triangular trademark. A London agent was engaged, Mr George Greenshields MacWilliam, and from his showrooms in Bartlett's Buildings, Holborn, Maling's began to court the all important 'buyers' for the big London china shops and department stores.

London agents were vitally important to provincial potteries. Although Staffordshire was the centre of pottery manufacturing, the centre of the pottery trade was undoubtedly London. The Holborn district was crammed with pottery showrooms and it was here, rather than at the potteries, that buyers from both home and abroad made their choices and placed their orders. The 'trade paper' for the buyers, *The Pottery Gazette*, was published from an address in Holborn and an important part of the London agent's work was to keep the profile of the firm high in this very influential journal. No doubt acting on Mr MacWilliam's advice, Maling's began to place regular monthly advertisements in *The Pottery Gazette* and these must have helped considerably in establishing the name of Maling in the minds of the buyers.

By the 1890s Maling advertisements in *The Pottery Gazette* were emphasising what was to become one of the firm's hallmarks: the wide range of their productions. They were manufacturers of 'every description of superior earthenware' from jars for wholesale jam manufacturers to smartly printed dinner services. The diversity of their productions is also reflected in the 106 patents of design that the firm took out between 1886 and 1917. These patents covered a wide variety of items: shapes of surgical dishes, urinals, pudding basins; decorative shapes for ornate tea pots; decorative printed patterns, both in single colours and multicoloured lithographs. The only patent of invention taken out during this period was in 1890 (patent no.8917) which covered a method of making standard capacity mugs or jars by inserting a suitable amount of filling (either soft glaze or Cornish

1.16

stone) into a vessel to bring it down to the correct capacity. There was some debate between C.T. Maling, G.G. MacWilliam and the firm's lawyers as to whether this patent contravened an earlier patent taken out by Tams Ltd., a Staffordshire firm, but the problems were eventually resolved.

Cetem Ware

During the 1890s the production of decorated table ware grew ever stronger. New shapes and patterns were introduced; a new department was established at the Ford Pottery to produce colour lithographs under the direction of a Mr. Miguet. The death in 1901 of C.T. Maling did not affect this expansion and the activity culminated in 1908 with the launch of a new range of dinner, toilet, tea and breakfast services under the trademark of Cetem Ware. Cetem Ware was promoted as a 'superior semi-porcelain, brilliant and durable' and the pottery made much of its whiteness, attributed to a special white body and 'a process of their own which gives the goods a china like appearance'.

Cetem Ware was good quality, sensible earthenware for the middle classes with 'original and up to date' shapes and decoration, largely the work of the firm's new designer, Harry Clifford Toft, who arrived at the Ford Pottery from Staffordshire in 1908. Toft was a pottery painter from a well known Staffordshire family. His uncles, Charles and Joseph Toft, were both respected Wedgwood decorators and Harry was also related to the eminent Victorian sculptor Albert Toft. The employment of an established commercial designer from Staffordshire underlines the Malings' determination to succeed in the market for domestic pottery, a market where decoration was as important a selling point as cheapness.

Another important acquisition was the new London agent, Mr. S. Stanley, who replaced George MacWilliam on the latter's death in 1910. Stanley had himself been a London buyer, and he brought with him invaluable connections in the London trade. He also seems to have brought practical suggestions. In 1910 *The Pottery Gazette* noted that some of the new shapes and designs in Maling ranges 'were, we understand, suggested by Mr. Stanley especially for the home trade, the requirements of which he is familiar'. One of the most useful of Stanley's connections was the close relationship he appears to have enjoyed with *The Pottery Gazette*. From the beginning of his agency in 1910 until his death in 1935 Maling's received consistently strong coverage in the 'Buyer's Notes' section of the journal

1.17

1.20

1.16 The showroom at the Ford B Pottery, photographed by *The Pottery Gazette* in 1916.
1.17 A group of women 'fettlers', smoothing off the wares with sponges on a lathe in the topping and turning shop; photograph taken by F.T. Maling c. 1915-1920 (PC).
1.20 A group of the staff on the pottery's footbridge, photograph taken in October 1920 (PC).

which provided comment on new lines brought out by potteries. The comments on Maling pottery were invariably so enthusiastic about the usefulness, saleability and overall excellence of the wares that it is tempting to wonder whether they were actually written by Stanley himself!

As the production of Cetem Ware expanded so did the decorating departments in the potteries. Some of the decorators, like Toft, were 'imported' from Staffordshire; among these were the two women who oversaw the painting department, Miss Williams and Miss Betty Jackson (who was, according to one of her charges, 'a holy terror'). Others were drawn from local families. The firm's engravers, Fred Wheater, Ben Gumley and, from 1926, Cecil Parker, were locally born, as was the works manager, Mr. Cartledge (also 'a terror' to all accounts). Most of the paintresses were local and usually acquired their jobs because of some previous family connection with the pottery. Lily Fordham, for instance, who started as a paintress in 1919 was the daughter of Mrs. Forster, the pottery's cook, who also had the exhausting task of laundering all the paintresses' pinafores every day. Lily Spearman who became a paintress in 1906 was the daughter of Mrs. Spearman, who held a 'licence to peddle' from the pottery, making her living selling Maling pottery door to door in Newcastle.

1.18

The paintresses worked in groups of four sitting on benches around a table with china 'tablets' in which to mix their colours. Other girls were employed as the 'blowers', putting the coloured background colours on to the wares by pressurised air guns; or stencillers, blocking out the printed areas prior to blowing with 'a red powder mixed with vinegar'. The red powder may have been some form of red lead since the girls had to wear masks while they were working; eventually the red powder was done away with and the patterns were blocked out by a thin layer of liquid slip.

The 1920s : Maling Ware

Cetem Ware was successful and it laid the foundations for the 1920s, probably the most interesting decade in the pottery's history. Toft died in 1922 but he was replaced as head designer by C.N. Wright, another established pottery painter who had worked at Wedgwood and Doulton. Wright was joined in 1926 by Lucien Boullemier, the son of the famous Minton painter Antonin Boullemier, and the pottery's best known designer (see chapter 4). The 1920s saw the introduction of new types of 'fancy goods', a new trademark – the famous Maling Ware castle, a new London showroom and expansion into new overseas markets with the opening of showrooms in Australia, New Zealand and Copenhagen.

1.19

The 1920s also saw considerable public acclaim in their home town, thanks largely to the Malings' connections with the ebullient Arthur Lambert, twice Lord Mayor of Newcastle and the inspiration behind the 1929 North East Coast Exhibition. Arthur Lambert was the owner of Townsend's China Galleries, Newcastle's best china shop, and an enthusiastic public speaker on 'The Art of the Potter'. His terms of office created many opportunities to promote Newcastle's very own pottery, culminating in an official Mayoral visit to the Ford Pottery in 1927 during which he waxed eloquent about the 'lustre' that the firm was bringing to Tyneside (fig. 1.21). During the visit Lambert was presented with a portrait of himself painted by Lucien Boullemier, not, unfortunately, on a piece of Maling pottery but on a piece of Doulton china.

Improvements to the pottery continued during the 1920s and by the time that the Newcastle and Gateshead Chamber of Commerce wrote a profile of the firm in their 1927 Journal, the pottery was entirely powered by electricity (in 1890 the Ford B Pottery had been one of the first English potteries to install electric light). The adoption of electric power had probably been encouraged by the firm's experiences during the General Strike of 1926 which had severely disrupted supplies of coal from Walbottle collieries.

However, beneath the surface matters were not quite so assured. Competition from abroad continued to trouble all English potteries, and the trade situation was certainly not helped by the general trade depression and the General Strike, during which the Ford A Pottery was forced to close. On the financial side, additional uncertainty was provided by the death in 1924 of John Ford Maling (fig. 1.22), the eldest of the three brothers who had had charge of the Ford A Pottery. His shares were eventually acquired by the two remaining brothers but after some uncertainty.

In 1930, the two remaining Malings decided to put the firm's long term finances on a firmer footing by turning the concern into a limited company. C.T. Maling & Sons Ltd. was registered in December 1930 as a private company with a registered capital of £25,000. C.T. Maling was to be the Managing Director of the new company and both he and his brother were to remain permanently on the board so long as they continued to hold at least 500 shares each. For the first time in the firm's history, directors from outside the family circle were brought in, but these two

1.21

'outsiders' were in fact family friends: Sir Alfred Appelby, and the Malings' solicitor, C.D. Bean.

The restructuring of the company appears to have given the firm a fresh financial start and C.T. Maling & Sons Ltd. entered the 1930s still in relatively buoyant mood. The pottery's products continued to keep abreast of changing fashions, and although the firm lost its famous designer Lucien Boullemier in 1936, his son Lucien George Boullemier, who had come to Newcastle from Wood Bros. in Staffordshire in 1933, proved a capable replacement. Another arrival from Staffordshire was the modeller Norman Carling who came from Wilkinson's in 1935 and whose talents enabled Maling's to produce some of their most novel ranges of 'fancies'.

The 1930s saw considerable changes on the personnel side. 1933 saw the death of the firm's invaluable London agent, S. Stanley, followed in 1934 by the death of the Managing Director, C.T. Maling; he had proved a worthy successor to his father and was famous for his long working day at the pottery, often arriving at 6 in the morning and leaving late at night. This loss was followed in February 1935 by the untimely death of John Cherry, the pottery's manager, and finally in 1937 the death of F.T. Maling, the last surviving son of the grand old man. The fortunes of the firm now lay largely with the trustees of the two brothers, and the Board of Directors which, for the first time, included no member of the Maling family.

The 1930s proved to be a difficult decade. Trade continued to be depressed in

1.22

1.18 Another group of women, probably fettlers; photograph taken by F.T. Maling, c. 1915-1920 (PC).
1.19 Mrs Fairlamb and two unidentified women probably checking wares before glazing; photograph taken by F.T. Maling c. 1915-1920 (PC).
1.21 Arthur Lambert's visit to the Ford Pottery in October 1927, during his term as Lord Mayor of Newcastle. F.T. Maling stands on his right, C.T. Maling on his left.
1.22 John Ford Maling (1858-1924). John Ford Maling had charge of the Ford A Pottery (PC).

the unpredictable home market. A lot of money was said to have been lost in 1936 thanks to the unexpected abdication of Edward VIII only weeks before his coronation: Maling's, like all British pottery firms, had produced large quantities of coronation souvenirs well in advance in anticipation of healthy sales during the celebrations. By 1938, however, recovery seemed to be on the way, as the *Evening Chronicle* reported:

> 'There is no denying that the firm felt the trade depression seriously.....
> It was a struggle to weather it, but they did so and were prepared to
> face the present period in which people seem to have money not only
> for essential earthenware articles, but for the decorative items which
> are the charm, if not the bread and butter of the industry.'

These hopes of a recovery were dashed with the outbreak of war in 1939 which took many of the Ford Pottery's workers away to the forces and brought in Government regulated production. Pottery was classed as an 'essential industry' but production was concentrated into certain licensed factories. Maling's were one of the firms fortunate enough to be given a licence but the quantities and type of pottery produced were strictly curtailed. The manufacture of decorated ware was restricted to export orders only (in order to earn foreign currency) but the home market had to make do with plain white or ivory 'utility ware', the size, range and price of which were all set by government regulations according to which 'group' the firm was put into. Maling's were in Group 1 for most utility articles but Group CZ for jugs.

It proved difficult to resume normal production after the war, largely because of the depleted workforce. As an 'out pottery' the company always found it far more difficult than their competitors in Staffordshire to recruit people with the necessary skills, and even as late as 1948 they were still trying to encourage back old members of the workforce who had left during the war. On the technological side, the Ford Pottery was also beginning to suffer from its by now old fashioned manufacturing processes. Some idea of the degree to which the Ford Pottery had fallen behind the times by the late 1940s comes from a report produced in January

1.23

1948 and probably written by a representative of the Staffordshire firm Wilkinsons, acting on behalf of the British Ceramic Manufacturers' Federation.

According to this very detailed report, every stage of the manufacturing process needed improvements: materials were not kept to a consistent standard; the casting plant was 'not what we call a modern casting plant'; practically all the hollow ware was still being turned on the jigger by hand rather than by machine, an old fashioned and expensive way of making pottery that was no longer used in Staffordshire 'except for the very highest class ware'. Particular criticism was made of the pottery's failure to pack the biscuit and glost (glaze) ovens to their full capacity; in the case of the glost ovens, the fault was inexcusable since 'at the present time (you) are paying for biscuit ware to be transported to Stoke on Trent to be glazed and fired for you and transported back, when in my opinion you could fire all the biscuit ware you can possibly make, in your glost ovens as you have presently got them'. The decorating departments escaped severe criticism except to say that the standard of glazing 'would not be satisfactory if times were competitive'.

The report's concluding paragraphs, under the heading 'General Observations and Outlook', must have made particularly painful reading. Since the 1880s Maling's had always taken great pride in the wide range of pottery that they produced, but now this was a matter for criticism:

> 'I am of the opinion that for the output you are presently doing you are making far too many articles..... As I told you, I should be inclined to call for a list of every article that is being made, classify them according to your costs and selling value, and determine which are the least remunerative and cut these articles out..... you have got to establish whether you are going to make everything for everybody or whether you are going to be a speciality house, concentrating upon certain lines of articles which you can make at that factory, and rigorously refuse to be sidetracked with regard to other types of articles which you are not in a favourable position to manufacture'.

The diversity that had once been one of the firm's major assets had now turned into a handicap.

This report must have made depressing reading for the firm's directors which by January 1948 were headed by the pottery's new owners. The previous August the trustees of the late F.T. and C.T. Maling had decided that any recovery would need 'outside money', and they had accordingly sold the pottery premises to Hoult's, the rapidly expanding Tyneside firm of furniture removers. The board of C.T. Maling & Sons was now headed by James Hoult, one of the three brothers who had founded Hoult's Removals Ltd., and the new Managing Director was another brother, Frederick Hoult. According to some of the Ford Pottery's employees at the time, the take over came as a complete surprise. The first they heard of it was one Saturday morning when they were all invited into the boardroom to meet the new directors.

At first sight the Hoult brothers' interest in the pottery is surprising: pottery manufacturing and furniture removals could not be further apart. However, there were already personal connections between the Hoults and the Malings, and the acquisition of the pottery also made good commercial sense in that the large site of the Ford B Pottery was just what the Hoults needed in order to 'rationalise' their many different furniture repositories scattered all over Newcastle. By the late 1940s less than half of the premises was being used for pottery production and the unused portion provided Hoult's with ample storage space and garaging for their increasingly large fleet of lorries.

1.24

1.23 Decorators at the Ford Pottery in September 1936 (Photograph courtesy Newcastle Chronicle and Journal Ltd.)
1.24 Advertisement for Maling White Ware, January 1937, photograph from *The Pottery Gazette*.

The Hoult's period.

Fortunately for the pottery's workforce, Frederick Hoult, the new Managing Director, took a sympathetic view of the pottery's potential. It was he who had commissioned the report from the British Ceramic Manufacturers' Federation early in 1948 and he soon began to put many of its recommendations into practice. New equipment was installed; the pottery's Assistant Manager, Les Dixon, was sent to Staffordshire to be taught a more scientific approach to pottery production, and a successful export drive was embarked upon. Frederick Hoult's aim, according to an article in the *Weekly Chronicle* in 1948, was 'to bring back to Maling pottery the proud position it formerly held in the forefront of the industry throughout the world'.

By 1952 his efforts appeared to be paying results. According to a profile of the firm in *The Pottery Gazette*, Maling's had a 'bright future' in front of them. More new equipment had recently been installed, including a Birlec tunnel kiln, automatic electric furnaces and four new filter presses. Although the workforce still stood at 250, a quarter of its full capacity, production levels were reasonably healthy and the firm was securing good orders in three areas of the pottery market: domestic goods, decorated fancies, and hospital and canteen wares. By this time the firm had indeed reduced its ranges and instead of the variety of decorative effects that the pre-war period had seen, Maling's now concentrated just on brightly coloured lustre pieces.

The Ford Pottery's recovery received a setback with the death of Fred Hoult in 1954. The 1950s was a time of further expansion on the furniture removal front and the remaining Directors were unable to devote the time and effort to the pottery that was really required. More importantly, the increasingly severe foreign competition, now not only from Europe and America but also from the Far East, threw an increasingly ominous shadow over the pottery's 'bright future'. Maling's had a vivid illustration of the strength of this new foreign competition when they lost the contract to supply crockery to the London and North Eastern Railway Company. The new contract went to a Japanese firm who proved able to supply exactly the same goods but at a quarter of the prices.

By the early 1960s Maling pottery was no longer a profitable commodity and the final blow came in 1962 when the firm lost its contract with Ringtons, a contract

1.26

1.27

1.28

1.25 Maling's London showroom in June 1939, photograph taken by *The Pottery Gazette*.
1.26 Display of Maling's lustre pottery in Fenwicks probably in the early 1950s (F).
1.27 A smart Fenwick's window display of Maling pottery, probably from the late 1950s (F).
1.28 Lucien George Boullemier, the pottery's designer from 1932, photographed in 1989 holding an experimental matt glazed bowl from the late 1950s (photograph courtesy Mr T. Boullemier).

that had provided a steady and reliable source of income since the 1920s. In June 1963 the Ford Pottery's gates were finally closed, bringing to an end 201 years of pottery production under the Maling name, and marking almost to the day the 157th anniversary of the firing of the first kiln at the Ouseburn Bridge Pottery. The headline carrying the story in *The Journal* read 'competition kills city firm' and the report included a sad quote from one of C.T. Maling & Sons' longest serving employees, the 73 year old gatekeeper, John Routledge: 'I've known this company since I was a nipper. What a great pity it is to see them go'.

2.2

Chapter 2

The early wares, 1762 to the 1880s

The most elusive type of pottery for the present day Maling collector is the 18th century pottery produced at the North Hylton pot works. The Malings occupied this pottery for over 50 years but as yet not one marked example of its products has come to light. However, some clues to the possible appearance of John Maling's North Hylton pots can be found in two unmarked creamware mugs in Sunderland Museum (fig. 2.1), both of which have been attributed to North Hylton on the basis of provenance (past ownership). The mugs are typical pieces of late 18th century creamware, hand painted with flowers surrounding a rather laboriously lettered inscription which, on one, is dated 1793. The distinctive decoration has been used to attribute a few further creamware mugs to the North Hylton pottery.[1]

Another clue to the nature of the Malings' North Hylton pots can be found in the day books of the famous Newcastle engraving workshop owned by Ralph Beilby and Thomas Bewick. The Malings are said to have been the first North East pottery manufacturers to use the technique of transfer printing, that is decorating pottery by means of a printed image taken from an engraved copper plate, and the Beilby Bewick workshop records confirm that the pottery was ordering copper printing plates from 1778 onwards. Fortunately the records name some of these early patterns:[2] The Nankin pattern, 1788; Jack on a Cruise, 1788; Masonic designs, 1788; The Miller (or old man), his son and their ass, 1788; A large ship for pots, 1788; View of the Grange, 1789; Crests, 1792; Doves, 1796; View of Sunderland Bridge for pint pots, 1797. Unfortunately no actual pieces of pottery bearing these

2.1

2.1 Two creamware mugs attributed to the North Hylton Pottery, 1790s (Sunderland Museum and Art Gallery: Tyne and Wear Museums Service).
2.2 Creamware plate with a printed verse and handpainted flowers mainly in iron red and green, named and dated 1828, M1.1 (GW).

patterns have been convincingly identified as pieces of 18th century Maling.

Maling pottery from the first half of the nineteenth century is slightly less elusive thanks to the introduction of back stamping, that is marking pottery on the back of the piece with the maker's name. The earliest Maling mark consists of the name Maling impressed in a semi-circle, and it has always been assumed, although not proven, that this mark was only introduced after the pottery moved to the Ouseburn Bridge in Newcastle in 1817; the mark is certainly the style used by several other Tyneside potteries of the period. A few pieces of creamware and pearlware with this semi-circular mark are known, among them two creamware plates with the useful addition of a date (fig. 2.2, plates A, B). If both these dated pieces are typical of the Ouseburn Bridge's productions in the late 1820s they suggest that the pottery was a rather old fashioned one, producing a type of pottery that had not substantially altered since the late 18th century; the print of the ship on one of the 1828 plates could even perhaps be the 'large ship' supplied by the Beilby Bewick workshop in 1788.

Like many early 19th century potters the Malings used pink lustre to add a touch of decorative glamour to their printed creamware. The lustre bordered plaques in figure 2.3 are all marked with the semi-circular mark, as is a similar plaque in Sunderland Museum (illustrated MTP). The cheerful green and yellow dash borders which surround the sober messages on these plaques are sometimes found on unmarked pink lustre mugs and jugs printed with views of the Sunderland Bridge, and it has been suggested that these may also be Maling pieces rather than Sunderland ones.

Pink lustre was also used in the cheap and cheerful hand painted patterns known as Gaudy Welsh or Gaudy Dutch. Several pieces of marked Maling Gaudy Welsh are known, of which the most interesting is a teapot with an elaborately moulded, rather porcelain-like shape (plate C)[3]. Although many Gaudy Welsh pieces appear to be decorated at random, the Malings used at least two patterns, both of which can be seen on the pieces in figure 2.4.

As the 19th century progressed the technique of transfer printing came to dominate pottery decoration and the Ouseburn Bridge Pottery was no exception. Robert Maling appears to have used quite standard pottery prints for the period Oriental patterns, popular genre scenes and typographical views such as the Denon's Egypt series, taken from the published engravings of Baron Dominique Denon who accompanied Napoleon on his Egyptian campaign. Several views made up the series, all of which have some Egyptian element – an obelisk, a pyramid or an Egyptian boat (fig. 2.5). The pattern was one that was used by other potters and

2.3

2.5

2.4

2.6

2.3 Two pearlware plaques with pink lustre borders, printed inscription with green and yellow painted dashes, c.1820-30, M.1.1 (SM).
2.4 Group of Gaudy Welsh patterns 1830-50; the mug is dated 1845, M1.3 (SM).
2.5 Pickle dish, blue printed Denon's Egypt pattern, 1830-50, M1.3 (PC).
2.6 Plaque, printed with one of the 'Poor Richard' series, 1830-50, M1.4 (photograph courtesy Mr. and Mrs. Upton).
2.7 Three printed plates c.1820-50, all M1.1 with M1.2 on the larger plate. The print of Oriental birds is similar to Ridgway's 'Persian' pattern (SM, LAG).
2.8 Daisy plate with black printed Chinese Beggar pattern, 1850s, M1.7 (SM).

2.8

2.7

Robert Maling may have bought the plates from one of the commercial pottery engravers in Staffordshire. Most blue printed Denon's Egypt pieces seem to date from the 1840s or 1850s but some cruder versions of the design, printed in green or black, were issued later in the century (TP illustrates an 1889 bowl).

Another mid-nineteenth century series of prints which the pottery re-issued later in its lifetime was the 'Poor Richard's Way to Wealth' series, a popular moral tale taken from Dr. Franklin's Maxims. Besides the plaque illustrated in figure 2.6, a daisy plate showing Poor Richard selling his cow is known. Both pieces are impressed with the Robert Maling mark (appendix 1.4) which was probably used in the 1830s and 1840s. The Poor Richard series was to be re-issued in the 1950s and the illustration of these 'Victorian Reproductions' (fig. 8.4) shows some of the other scenes in the series. Other printed patterns used in the early and mid

2.9

2.10

nineteenth century include the ubiquitous willow pattern and a variety of fairly typical Oriental flavoured prints. (figs. 2.7, 2.8, 2.9); the pieces in figs. 2.8 and 2.9 are all impressed C.T. Maling and therefore post-date 1853, when he took over the management of the pottery from his father.

Also from the 1850s are the patterns on an engraved copper plate which was given to the Laing Art Gallery in 1938 by Frederick Maling (fig. 2.10). This plate includes several familiar patterns – a Crimean war commemorative and the popular Sailor's Farewell and Sailor's Return – all of which can be found on pieces from other north-east potteries. C.T. Maling's use of these prints is, however, confirmed by a pink lustre bowl which bears the Crimea print and an impressed mark (fig. 2.11). A second copper plate from the same source is engraved with earlier looking patterns, vignettes on the theme of 'Mama's Musical Trio' taken from the pretty neo-classical engravings of Adam Buck. No fully marked piece of Maling pottery with these patterns has been recorded but several unmarked pieces have been attributed to the Ouseburn Bridge Pottery on the basis of this copper plate[4].

Maling's engraver from 1926 until 1946, Cecil Parker, remembers that the pottery kept a large collection of old 19th century copper printing plates, some of which were occasionally dusted off and re-used. This certainly happened to the Poor Richard plates, and some other 20th century patterns also have a distinctly 19th century look to them: notably the Venetian Scenes (fig. 8.3), the Ming and Blue Egypt patterns (both illustrated TP). Some pieces from the late 19th century may also re-use prints of a slightly earlier date. For instance, the Rich Lady jug (fig. 2.12) bears the triangular trade mark introduced in 1885 but the print matches the similar huntsmen print found on a jug and mug (fig. 2.13), bearing the printed mark 'RM'.

The pieces in fig. 2.13 are good illustrations of a general truth about early Maling pottery, which is that towards the middle of the nineteenth century the quality appears to decline. The early creamware plates are often thin and delicately potted but towards the middle of the century the bodies get thicker and the prints are often clumsily applied. By the 1850s Maling pottery seems to bear out the truth of a comment made in a local directory of 1855: 'the potteries of the Tyne do not aim at the dainty and the tasteful, they are content with the useful. Their pots have to bear rough usage and they are made roughly'.

2.9 Three printed patterns of the 1850s, all M1.7 with M1.9 on the larger plate (LAG, SM).
2.10 Pull from a Maling copper plate of the 1850s (LAG).
2.11 Bowl, pink lustre with printed Crimea patterns, mid 1850s, M1.7 (Dr. and Mrs. C. Bell)
2.12 Exeter shape jug printed with the 'Rich Lady' pattern, 1880s, but probably using an earlier print, M1.11 (SM).
2.13 Jug and mug printed with the Huntsman pattern, 1840-1850?, M1.8 on mug (SM).
2.14 Teapot said to be the first teapot made by machinery at the Ford A Pottery, the label reads "The first machine teapot. Made February/60" (PC).

2.12

2.11

2.14

2.13

Footnotes:

1. See *Creamware and Pearlware*, catalogue of the 5th Northern Ceramic Society Exhibition, Stoke on Trent City Museums, 1986, pp. 42, 43, 72. Sunderland Museum has several similarly decorated mugs attributed to North Hylton.

2. 'The Potteries of Tyne and Wear, and their dealings with the Beilby Bewick workshop', M.A.V. Gill, in *Archaeologia Aeliana*, 5th series, vol.IV, 1976, pp. 151 – 170.

3. An unmarked coffee pot of matching shape decorated with a print of a Danish scene is illustrated in an article by Mogens Bencard on English pottery decorated for the Danish market. In the journal *Mark og Montre*, 1976, p. 85.

4. 'Adam Buck on Ceramics', C. Williams Wood, *Apollo*, June 1985, pp. 395 – 402; this article illustrates the copper plate.

Throughout the period of the Ouseburn Bridge and the Ford A potteries, the Malings were producing table ware rather than ornamental ware. Shapes tended to be basic with two exceptions, both teapots: one is the porcelain shaped teapot illustrated in plate C; the other is illustrated in figure 2.14 and is said to have been the first teapot to have been made with machinery at the Ford A Pottery. According to C.T. Maling's evidence to the Children's Employment Commission of 1863, he was producing teapots, cups, jugs and bowls with machinery and it is intriguing to wonder whether he was referring to quite decorative moulded tableware of this type rather than plain ordinary vessels of the type illustrated in figure 2.13. The Ford A teapot, and the equally intriguing jug made in 1878 (fig. 3.1) are useful reminders that our knowledge of Maling pottery during the first 120 years of its production is still very limited.

3.3

Chapter 3

The 1880s to 1920: new designs and Cetem Ware

New printed patterns

The new patterns introduced in the 1880s were more consciously 'artistic' than the traditional printed patterns that had been used hitherto. A good example of the new fashions in pottery prints is the Poachers pattern, probably from the early 1880s (fig. 3.2). It is absolutely typical of popular 'artistic' pottery of the period with a brown printed motif set asymmetrically in a reserved twiggy panel on an ivory body. Patterns such as this were popular English versions of the Japanese designs which had had a strong influence on western design from the 1860s onwards, and the Malings underlined their awareness of this fashionable artistic interest by naming a pattern of 1885 Japan (fig. 3.2). In fact the Japan pattern is rather a conventional looking pottery print consisting, like many earlier pottery prints, of a large central motif of Oriental vases. The only thing that marks it out as an 1880s design rather than an 1830s one is its thin geometric border.

The new fashionable 1880s patterns were printed on a new ivory coloured body, another element in the new 'artistic' image of 1880s Maling. New shapes were introduced to go with the new patterns, and sometimes the combination of an artistic print, ivory body, and smart new shape could produce something quite stylish, such as the Kilda pattern tureens of the late 1880s (fig. 3.3).

The 1890s brought in new fashions in pottery prints, and in the case of C.T. Maling & Sons this meant patterns where bold sprays of realistic flowers and foliage wound artistically over the body of the piece: the patterns in figure 3.5 are all good

3.1

3.2

3.1 Jug said to be made from clay taken from the foundations of the Ford B Pottery, 1878; the label reads "this jug was made out of clay dug out of the foundations when B Ford Pottery was gitting (sic) built. Clay taken to A Ford Pottery, made there, fired and dipt in ordinary glaze" (PC).
3.2 Two printed patterns of the 1880s: left, Poachers; right, 'Japan' (SM).
3.3 Two tureens, 'Kilda' pattern registered in 1888, M1.11 plus indecipherable impressed registration number, probably for the shape, on the rounded tureen (LAG).

26

3.5

3.4

3.6

3.8

3.7

examples of this style. These 1890s floral prints are invariably very well engraved with lots of delicate stippling to indicate texture and shade. Since many of the patterns were registered in Maling's name (see appendix, section 3.6) the prints must have been designed and engraved 'in house'.

Around 1900 Maling tableware prints seem to undergo another alteration in style. The artistically winding floral prints give way to dainty border designs with ribbons and neo-classical swags: the Keswick and Blagdon patterns, both of 1901, are good examples and both anticipate the styles that were to dominate the Cetem Ware ranges of 1908 (both illustrated MTP). The change of style may have been a consequence of the introduction of a new white body, the 'superior semi-porcelain', or 'S.S.', body which was introduced in the late 1890s. This new white body represented a definite attempt to imitate porcelain and it was used for Maling's better quality pieces. Cheaper wares decorated with more traditional patterns, such as Asiatic Pheasants and Denon's Egypt, continued to be produced on the cream coloured, or 'C.C.', body.

Ornamental designs could be more ambitious than table ware patterns and the late nineteenth century saw some quite interesting blue printed designs on ornamental pieces. Among these are the Eversley pattern (fig. 3.7), and a print of apple

3.4 Saucer, 'Warwick' pattern, 1880s, M1.11 (SAG).
3.5 1890s floral patterns: large Durham shape tureen in 'Jesmond' pattern registered in 1893; small tureen in 'Ford' pattern; soup plate in 'Argyle' pattern, all M1.11, M1.12 (SM, LAG).
3.6 Plaque with floral print, year letters for 1889, M1.12. Interestingly this pattern is identical to the Kirkwood pattern issued by Royal Doulton in the 1930s (SM).
3.7 Vase, 'Eversley' pattern, c.1900, M1.11 (SM).
3.8 Plaque, printed pattern of apple pickers overpainted with a cobalt blue wash, M1.12 (SM).

Colour Plates

A Creamware plate, printed and handpainted, 1828, M1.1 (photograph courtesy Dr. and Mrs L. Rakow).
B Creamware plate, handpainted, 1830s, M1.3 (photograph courtesy the Rosalind and Martin Pulver Collection).
C Gaudy Welsh teapot, 1830-50, M1.3 (PC).
D Flask, 1906, pn 6336. M1.11 (SM).

A

B

C

D

pickers (fig. 3.8) which is an unusual example of a Maling pattern which includes figures.

Colour lithographs and rococo shapes

Maling pottery was no exception to the general trend in the 1890s towards more ostentatious decoration. Around 1895 a new building was erected on the far side of the Ford B Pottery to house the new decorating departments and here paintresses would give the pottery a slightly more ornate aspect by colouring in the prints with enamel colours. One basic pattern could thus be used to produce goods in three price ranges: basic, standard, or best quality. Basic would just consist of the plain printed pattern; standard would have the addition of one colour; best quality pieces would be gilded and lavishly painted using several colours (fig. 3.9).

Besides the new decorating department, the Ford Pottery also established a new lithography workshop. Chromo-lithographs enabled pottery manufacturers to produce pottery that was printed in more than one colour. It was a technique that had first been developed in the 1830s but was not fully adopted by the English pottery industry until the last quarter of the 19th century, under the pressure of competition from imported, cheaply decorated European porcelain. If the Ford Pottery had been in Staffordshire Maling's would probably have brought their colour lithographs from a specialist firm, such as Ratauds, but at least initially they produced their own, under a Frenchman called Mr. Miguet (figs. 3.10, 3.12). Maling's advertised that 'original chromo-lithographs (were) a speciality' and at least two designs were registered: the columbine border, and the green laurel wreath border registered in 1908 and seen on the 1911 coronation plate (both in fig. 3.17).

The production of colour lithographs was a long and costly business involving the preparation of several different stones, one for each colour that would be used in the design. Maling lithographs always look as though they originated as different layers of colour, unlike the later photographically produced lithographs which have a smooth and flat appearance. Although lithographs were printed in colour, the final piece was often given an additional hand painted finish to cover up any tiny mistakes, or to give the piece the appearance of a more costly hand painted article.

Another new decorative technique of the 1890s was the use of aerographed backgrounds, such as the peachy 'blush' seen on the pilgrim flask in colour plate D, one of a pair made as a Christmas present for an elderly aunt of Frederick Maling in 1906. This piece is a good example of the rather impressive effect that these new

3.9

3.11

3.9 Aberdeen sardine box, hand coloured 'Sylvia' print on an orange blush background, 1897, M1.12 plus impressed 'Rd. 306748', a registration number for 1897 which refers to the shape (PC).
3.10 Eden shape jug and flat plaque traveller's sample, colour lithographed c.1900; jug, pn 3182, M1.11 (SM).
3.11 Teapot design registered by Maling's in 1894, no. 225913 (photograph courtesy the Controller of Her Majesty's Stationery Office. Crown copyright. Public Record Office ref. BT50/204).

3.10

decorative techniques could produce. Every possible opportunity to add decoration has been taken: not only is the design colour lithographed, gilding and bronze edging has been applied and the whole pattern has been outlined with tube lining, a technique similar to icing a cake.

The counterpart to these new showy decorative techniques was the introduction of new showy rococo shapes. The most extreme examples are probably the shell tea pot registered in 1894 (fig. 3.11), the menu card (fig. 3.12), and the Britannia photograph frame of 1895 (illustrated TP). Toilet and tableware shapes were generally a little less extreme but the range of Eden shapes introduced around the turn of the century had shallow rococo 'embossments' around the scrolled edges of the pieces (fig. 3.13). These splendidly fussy shapes came from a long tradition of rococo pottery and porcelain which seems to have been eternally popular despite the disapproval of more high minded critics.

The Malings' determination to secure their place in the domestic market is underlined by the introduction of porcelain into their ranges. The porcelain they sold was not made at Newcastle, but imported in the white usually from a continental factory. On arrival at Newcastle it would be decorated with dainty colour lithographs and then resold with a Maling mark overstamped on top of the original producer's mark. The mark Maling's applied to this imported porcelain was different from the normal triangular mark in that it was a small picture of a castle. This is the first instance of Maling's using a castle as their trademark and it is interesting to speculate that the castle was chosen not for any sentimental reason but because it provided a solid block of ink which would cover up the 'Limoges France' mark beneath it.

The lithographs Maling's applied to porcelain tended to be much daintier and on a much smaller scale than the blowsy floral lithographs applied to pottery; tiny pink rosebuds were a great favourite. No doubt this smaller scale was designed to show off the delicate whiteness of the china body beneath and as the quality of the Ford Pottery's own productions improved so this daintier, smaller scale of decoration began to be used more on the home made pieces. It was, after all, pointless to cover up the attractions of the white and glossy superior semi-porcelain body with layers of aerographed coloured glazes and large coloured flowers. This tendency culminated in 1908 with the launch of a new range of designs under the trademark Cetem Ware.

Cetem Ware, 1908 – 1920

The name Cetem Ware and its sunburst trade mark were registered in 1908 and the new range of toilet and table ware was launched onto the market as a 'superior semi-porcelain, brilliant and durable, in the latest and most effective styles of decoration'. These latest styles were generally in the dainty china tradition of swags, and festoons in neat and tasteful border patterns (fig. 3.15). New plainer shapes were introduced (fig. 3.16) and these, as *The Pottery Gazette* noted in 1910, were 'suitable for receiving light and dainty designs emulative of china'. Much was made of the 'china-like appearance' of the new Cetem Ware.

Many of the new patterns were chromo-lithographs (fig. 3.17), but the best selling lines turned out to be the underglaze blue printed table ware (figs. 3.14, 3.16), particularly the Maltese pattern, introduced in 1911 and an immediate success according to *The Pottery Gazette* in 1913: 'the sales of this pattern which was introduced some twelve months ago have never flagged, indeed the demand since its initiation has been almost greater than the supply'. Maltese was originally available in either blue or green, with or without a gilded border. The Duchess border (fig. 3.24), registered in 1914, was equally successful and both patterns lasted the pottery well into the 1930s.

The success of Cetem Ware can be credited to two men: the firm's new designer, Harry C. Toft, and the firm's London agent from 1910, Mr. Stanley. It was probably thanks to Stanley's connections in the London trade that Cetem Ware seems to

3.12

3.13

3.14

3.17

2344. Granville Shape.

2358. Hylton Shape.

9532. Granville Shape.

2345. Dunlop Shape.

2346. Whitby Shape.

3.15

INDIAN BLUE "OBAN."
Albion Shape.

FLOWN MYRTLE "LEAFY."
Earl Shape.

3.16

3.12 Menu card, colour lithographed, year marks for 1898, pn 6169, M1.11 (KW).
3.13 Eden shape plate, printed and hand coloured, c.1900, M1.11 (KW).
3.14 Three underglaze blue prints for Cetem table ware, from left: 'Chelsea' registered in 1908; 'Maltese' registered in 1911; 'Empire' registered in 1908. All M1.17, M1.18 on Chelsea plate (PC, LAG, SAG).
3.15 Page from a 1920s catalogue showing earlier Cetem toilet ware patterns. The Whitby shape and pattern were registered in 1908 (SM).
3.16 Page from a 1920s catalogue showing earlier Cetem Ware table patterns. Oban was registered in 1913, the Earl shape was registered in 1908 (SM).
3.17 Group of colour lithographed pieces, from back: 'Columbine' plate, year marks from 1903, M1.11 with 'RD. PATTERN'; plate commemorating the 1911 coronation, M1.17; beaker with shamrock pattern c.1910, M1.17; toothbrush holder, c.1905, pn 7571, M1.11 with 'Manufactured for Harrod's Limited Brompton Rd. London.' The 1911 plate includes the words 'Harrod's Ltd. Exclusive Design' beneath the flags (LAG, SM).

have immediately found favour with Harrod's, the large London department store; many Cetem Ware items appear in Harrod's catalogues, along with C.T. Maling & Sons' more mundane kitchen and dairy pottery. The link with Harrod's was so strong that Maling's began to manufacture some items exclusively for the London store (fig. 3.17).

Initially Cetem Ware consisted of sets of matching toilet or table ware but soon new types of pottery began to appear. Nursery pottery was being made by 1910 (fig. 3.18), and by 1913 more ornamental items such as flower pots, bulb bowls and vases 'specially suitable for mounting with electric light fittings or with oil containers' were being promoted (fig. 3.19). Ornamental items demanded decoration that was a little less dainty and a little more glamorous and it was probably this need that led Maling's to develop a type of decoration for which they were to become famous: the black ground.

Black ground pottery set a hand coloured printed pattern against a glamorous black glazed background. Many other potteries produced black ground wares but according to *The Pottery Gazette* in 1920 Maling's were one of the pioneers:

One of the first houses to develop the all over black ground wares, C.T. Maling & Sons have lost none of their start in the matter, although many firms followed on their heels.

34

3.18

3.19

Black ground wares were first mentioned and illustrated in *The Pottery Gazette* in 1913 and the view of the pottery showroom in 1916 shows that black ground production was well under way by then (fig. 3.20). The smart new effect was immensely successful, particularly in the important London market. In 1927 Freddy Maling recalled an incident that had occurred 'shortly after they had started to make the celebrated black ware': a Tyneside woman, unable to buy the smart new toilet set that she wanted in her home town, travelled to London where she obtained one but was astonished to find, on receipt of the set, that it had been made in Newcastle.

The inspiration for black ground wares was undoubtedly the black and green Kang S'hi Chinese porcelain that was very fashionable at the time, and it is no surprise to find that many of the early black ground designs had an Oriental flavour. One of the earliest patterns, Poona (fig. 3.21), showed a tall vase with peonies and a Chinese fence. The stork, or Aquatic Birds pattern c.1918 (fig. 3.25) showed two storks surrounded by Chinese fluffy clouds: this was to be one of Maling's most

3.20

3.21

3.23

3.22

3.24

3.25

3.18 Nursery pottery, c.1910: 'Baby Plate', pn 8811, M1.11; Granville shape ewer with lithographs of pixies, M1.17 (KW).
3.19 No. 4 shape vase adapted as a lamp base, c.1913, pn 2344, M1.17 (LAG).
3.20 The Ford Pottery Showroom, from *The Pottery Gazette*, June 1916.
3.21 Lowestoft shape teapot and jug, c.1910 'Poona' pattern, pn 8639, M1.17 (SM).
3.22 Garniture of three vases c.1913, pn 9480. The central stand is also a piece of Maling pottery and is marked M1.17 (vases courtesy Ian Sharp Antiques, stand SM).
3.23 Tudor shape bowl with Owl pattern, c.1913, pn 9351, M1.17 (SM).
3.24 Plate with coloured print of Lloyd George as Minister of Munitions in the cabinet of May 1915 – July 1916. 'Duchess' blue printed border registered in 1914, M1.17 (LAG).
3.25 Page from a 1920s catalogue showing the earlier Acquatic Birds pattern, first used c.1918, in various colour combinations (SM).

serviceable patterns and it was redrawn, recoloured and reworked countless times during the 1920s and 1930s. Some exceptions to the Oriental rule are the rosebud vases (plate E), an uneasy classical pattern (plate F), and the curious plate with the caricature of Lloyd George as Minister of Munitions in the May 1915 War Cabinet (fig. 3.24).

Black ground wares were to be one of C.T. Maling & Sons' most enduring successes and the technique laid a firm foundation for the next advance, into the lucrative 'fancy goods' market of the 1920s.

4.1

Chapter 4

The 1920s: new colours and Maling Ware

The 1920s was one of the liveliest periods in C.T. Maling & Sons' history and the decade opened with the firm in buoyant mood as they moved the London showroom to a new address at Holborn Viaduct. Here, as *The Pottery Gazette* reported enthusiastically in 1920, the trade buyer could find:

> ...no brighter, prettier or more effective display of ornamental earthenware than that being shown by this old established house... The writer has seen the productions of C.T. Maling & Sons shown with vigour and confidence in many of the principal West End china emporiums, and shown, moreover, alongside some of the most reputed Staffordshire wares and if the goods can hold their own in that exclusive atmosphere it does not seem too much to argue that they could do the same anywhere.

The article reported that the firm was 'blocked with orders'.

The two pieces used to illustrate this report were two 'smart new bowls for table decoration', photographed with an arrangement of carnations and poppies. The flower bowl was one of the most important types of pottery for the 1920s pottery manufacturer, particularly the shallow 'floating bowl' in which cut flower heads could be delicately floated on water. Floating bowls were all the rage in the early 1920s and Maling's according to *The Pottery Gazette* in 1923, enjoyed a particularly strong association with them:

> We believe that the Ford Potteries, Newcastle upon Tyne, were the pioneers of the floating bowl and they have had remarkable success with the whole of their patterns, and they are still making probably as many floating bowls as any house engaged in pottery manufacture.

The most popular floating bowl shape produced at the Ford Potteries was the shallow Sefton bowl introduced in 1922 (fig. 4.1).

Besides flower bowls (figs. 4.2, 4.3), Maling's introduced a number of other new types of 'fancies' into their ranges during the early 1920s; the term fancies seems to have been used to describe both ornamental ware and special table ware items. Maling fancies of the 1920s included bulb bowls, lampstands, chimney piece vases, cream cheese boxes, honey pots, salad bowls and cigarette boxes with matching ashtrays. *The Pottery Gazette* particularly recommended the latter to the china and earthenware dealer who 'is ever confronted with the problem of providing something that is fresh and useful for 'present wares''.

New patterns and shapes were introduced to go with these new types of goods, and, above all, there was a new emphasis on colour. Colour is a constant theme in *The Pottery Gazette*'s commentaries on Maling ranges of the 1920s: the 1920 bowls were 'treated in the new bright colours that are being so emphatically called for by all the best and most artistically minded furnishing houses'; in 1929, 'bril-

4.1 Sefton shape floating bowl, plum blossom, pn 2675, c.1922, M1.17 (SM).

Octagon Bowl, 3165
Lotus Bowl, 2829
Kenwood Bowl, 2889
Sefton Bowl, 3190
(on loose Black Stand)
Octagon Bowl (footed) 2868
Kenwood Bowl, 2856

Bulb Bowls.

4.2

4.3

liance of colour and a judicious placement of it seems to characterise quite the major proportion of patterns that are brought out by this house'. Black ground wares continued to be made but Maling's also began to introduce vividly coloured grounds (fig. 4.5, plate G). Pink, red, lime green, purple and that ubiquitous 1920s colour canary yellow (plate H), are all found as Maling ground colours during the 1920s.

Patterns were also updated. New patterns tended to be simpler and more stylised and by the middle of the decade the patterns, instead of covering the whole of the piece, had been pushed back to the rims. Good examples are the border patterns in figure 4.3 and the striking Milan border (fig. 4.4) which appears in an advertisement of 1924 and must be credited to the ex-Wedgwood painter C.N. Wright who arrived at Newcastle following the death of Harry Toft in 1922. Wright seems to have produced some of Maling's most stylish patterns, many of which consist of these simple yet strong border patterns set against boldly coloured grounds.

It was during Wright's time at the pottery that the firm introduced the Maling Ware trade mark. It first appears in an advertisement of July 1924 replacing the Cetem Ware mark that had appeared in the previous month's advertisement. The reason for the introduction of a new mark is not known. Maling Ware was not

4.4

4.5

promoted as a new range of designs and pieces from the change-over period bear the Maling Ware mark overstamped on top of the old Cetem Ware mark. Neither was Maling Ware meant to completely replace the Cetem Ware mark which continued to be used until the 1930s. The introduction of a new mark certainly suggests a wish to update the pottery's image but it seems to have been a low-key and gradual change that was spread out over several years. Wright appears to have stayed in Newcastle until 1928 when he returned to Staffordshire to take up a post with Keeling's, producers of 'Losol Ware'.

Lucien Boullemier

The changes introduced by C.N. Wright in the middle of the 1920s were continued by his successor, Lucien Boullemier (fig. 4.6) who was described as having 'recently left the Staffordshire potteries to take charge of the decorating departments at the Ford Potteries, Newcastle' in April 1926. Like his earlier predecessor, Toft, he came from a distinguished pottery family, his father Antonin having been one of Minton's best known French painters in the late nineteenth century. Lucien Emile Boullemier was born in 1877 in Stoke, and during his youth made quite a name for himself not in pottery but in football: while playing for Port Vale Football Club he had scored the winning goal against Sheffield United in the 1898 F.A. Cup. He eventually took up his father's profession and from 1900 to 1906 was working in America at the Lennox china factory in New Jersey. He returned to England to work first at Minton's but later at the Soho Pottery in Cobridge, from where he joined Maling's in 1926.

The Malings were quite excited about Boullemier, believing that they had pulled off rather a coup by enticing him away from Staffordshire. He was certainly their best known designer, memorable not only for his artistic skills but also for his colourful personality. He was a large, flamboyant and occasionally eccentric man who often dressed in a trilby and sang operatic arias as he worked. Singing was one of his great loves and this was another talent that he had inherited from his father who at one time had sung professionally with the Opera Comique in Paris. Boullemier was remembered by those who had worked with him not only as a 'character' but also as a 'nice chap'.

Boullemier's influence on the appearance of Maling pottery was considerable. His career up to 1926 had been largely spent decorating quite high class porcelain and he seems to have injected a new 'posh' element into his new firm. Under his direction many of the firm's existing designs were updated in rather glamorous

4.6

4.2 Page from a late 1920s catalogue showing bulb bowls with some pre-1920s patterns (SM).
4.3 Page from a late 1920s catalogue showing floating bowls with mid-1920s patterns (SM).
4.4 Kenwood shape yellow ground 'Milan' pattern bowl, 1924, pn 2856, M1.17 (LAG).
4.5 Page from a late 1920s catalogue showing morning sets in pink, red, yellow, green and purple coloured grounds, mid 1920s (SM).
4.6 Lucien Emile Boullemier (1877-1949), (photograph courtesy Mr L.G. Boullemier).

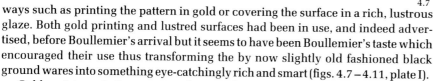

Sefton Bowl
3054

Lotus Bowl
3146

Octagon Bowl (footed)
3198

Sheldon Bowl (footed)
3063

Octagon Bowl
3196

Kenwood Bowl
3022

Stanley Bowl (footed)
3016

4.7

4.8

4.9

4.12

ways such as printing the pattern in gold or covering the surface in a rich, lustrous glaze. Both gold printing and lustred surfaces had been in use, and indeed advertised, before Boullemier's arrival but it seems to have been Boullemier's taste which encouraged their use thus transforming the by now slightly old fashioned black ground wares into something eye-catchingly rich and smart (figs. 4.7 – 4.11, plate I).

Gold register printing was a technique that Boullemier appears to have been particularly fond of. It was similar to ordinary transfer printing but the transfer would be applied using linseed oil rather than printing ink. The piece would be sprinkled with powdered gold which stuck only to the oiled areas and excess gold would be brushed off carefully so that as much gold as possible could be reused. The brushes and cloths were also carefully cleaned so that not a speck of gold would be wasted. A good example of the transformation that gold printing could effect is the 'Oriental' border pattern, introduced in 1924 as a simple underglaze blue tableware print (fig. 4.12) In Boullemier's hands the simple design is transformed into something far more lavish by being printed in gold and smothered with smart black and green enamel colouring (plate L).

Boullemier's arrival injected new glamorous life into old patterns and it also strengthened the return to Orientalism that had begun in the middle of the decade with the introduction of Japanese flavoured patterns featuring geisha girls, sinuous Satsuma dragons and gold brocade (fig. 4.8). These ornate, sometimes rather decadent looking, designs of the 1920s were very different to the pedestrian Chinese patterns which had been used on the early black ground wares. Under Boullemier's direction the firm also began the production of some very high quality lustre pieces (plates K, J). These luxurious lustre pieces shimmering with iridescent colour continued to be produced until Boullemier's departure in 1936. They are without doubt among C.T. Maling & Sons' most impressive productions, well able to stand comparison with the best that Staffordshire could produce at the time.

Gold printing and lustred surfaces are both characteristics of 'Boullemier period Maling'. A third feature of the pottery of the late 1920s was the breaking up of the flat solid colour backgrounds either by over-printing a gold brocade pattern, spraying on a mottled background, or hand painting a 'waved' background using short free hand brush strokes. This was not the first time that the pottery had used such textured backgrounds, the waved background is said to have been first used c.1910 in an attempt to imitate the 'crackled' ground on Oriental vases, but the use did not become extensive until the last half of the 1920s. The waved background was to become one of Maling pottery's most familiar characteristics and it featured heavily in the firm's designs right up to the 1950s (fig.7.13 shows some 1930s examples).

4.10

4.11

4.13

4.14

4.7 Page from a late 1920s catalogue showing Maling bowls with gold printed patterns (SM).
4.8 Gosforth shape jug c.1929, pn 3586, M1.23; geisha girls plate, c.1926, M1.23 (LAG, KW).
4.9 Cup and Saucer, late 1920s, M1.23 (SM).
4.10 Windmill pattern bowl, gold printed with thick overglaze colouring, c.1930?, M1.23 (PC).
4.11 Small Jazz shape bowl, early 1930s, pn 5225, M1.23 (SM).
4.12 1920s blue tableware prints: 'Oriental', 1924; 'Egypt', 1929. Both M1.23 (LAG).
4.13 Ogden's cigarette card no. 27 of the series 'Modern British Pottery' (SM).
4.14 Bowl, blue mottled ground and thick overglaze colouring, c.1932, pn 5669, M1.23 (FH).

Another technique that was introduced in the 1920s but which was to be heavily used in the future was the technique of embossing, in which the pattern would be outlined not by printing but by shallow raised lines which would then be filled in with colour. Embossed patterns were first illustrated in 1926 and, like the waved background, they increased the hand painted appearance of a piece of pottery, an increasingly important selling point in the 1920s. Although new blue printed tableware patterns were introduced during the decade (fig. 4.12) and colour lithographs continued to be used for some table ware, most Maling fancies had a printed or embossed pattern coloured in by hand. There is no doubt that this high proportion of hand painting helped to make Maling pottery of the 1920s stand out in a very advantageous way from many of its competitors.

The 1929 North East Exhibition, which will be looked at in the next chapter, provided a suitably exciting end to what had been an exciting decade for C.T. Maling & Sons. The decade had seen the successful culmination of their efforts to shake off their old image as producers only of jam jars, and a note in *The Pottery Gazette* of 1929 paid tribute to this achievement.

It is nothing short of marvellous how this house has managed to develop its activities from the manufacture of the veriest utilitarian undecorated ware, such as the common cream coloured jam jar up to a full range of dinner, tea and toilet ware, plus one of the most varied and brilliantly decorated range of fancies that has ever been placed before pottery retailers. From year to year over this past decade this firm's scope as regards the production of useful and decorative household pottery has been constantly widening, and the way in which they have managed to invade not only the domain of the retail establishment everywhere but to build up and consolidate a trade that was at one time well outside the original functions of their factory, is a story which, if it were told the way it deserves, would prove fascinating indeed.

Another tribute of a sort came when Maling pottery was included in the Ogden's cigarette card series, 'Modern British Pottery' (fig. 4.13). Maling vases featured on two cards in the series and the caption on the reverse praised what had now become the Newcastle pottery's hallmarks: 'brilliant, glowing colours and iridescent lustre enriched with gold'.

5.3

Chapter 5

The 1929 North East Coast Exhibition and Ringtons

The most important event on Tyneside during the summer of 1929 was the North East Coast Industries Exhibition which ran from May to October and attracted over 4 million visitors. The Exhibition was intended to be a show-case for North Eastern industries and it certainly fulfilled this aim well for C.T. Maling & Sons who were fortunate enough to be the sole representatives of an industry that was close to the heart of the Chairman of the event, the irrepressible Sir Arthur Lambert, owner of Townsend's China Galleries. The link between Townsend's and Maling's was underlined during the Exhibition by the fact the two firms shared a stand in the Palace of Industries. From this stand Townsend's sold Maling souvenirs of the Exhibition whilst the pottery's end of the stand had live demonstrations of pottery decorating (fig. 5.1).

Maling's produced several types of souvenir for the Exhibition, the best known of which is probably the 10 inch blue plaques which were sold at the time for 10s 6d (fig. 5.3). The plaque was designed by Boullemier and included a portrait of Arthur Lambert which was taken from the portrait Boullemier had painted for the

5.1 The stand shared by Townsend's and Maling's at the 1929 Exhibition.
5.3 Blue printed plaque commemorating the Exhibition, 1929, M1.23 with 'Townsend and Co.' (LAG).

5.1

5.2

5.4

5.5

then Lord Mayor two years earlier. The other elements in the design showed the major North East industries – engineering, ship building, coal mining and chemicals – surrounding a central view of the newly completed Tyne Bridge. This central view showed the pottery itself in the foreground and although it was shown on the wrong bank of the Tyne it must have pleased the pottery's workforce to see themselves linked to Tyneside's great and world famous industries. The central view of the Bridge is said to have been inspired by the view from Boullemier's studio window but although the bridge is certainly visible from the Ford Pottery, a lot of artistic licence has been employed to bring the two elements together when they are in fact two miles apart.

One small curiosity about these plaques is that two printed versions exist. On one the wording on the roof of the pottery buildings in the foreground reads 'Maling Ware', on the other it reads 'Maling Pottery'. The original engraved copper plate for the design is in the Laing Art Gallery and this definitely says 'Maling Pottery', suggesting that the other version may have been a later 'second edition'. A third

5.2 Blue printed Exhibition souvenirs, 1929, M1.22 (LAG).
5.4 Teacup and saucer commemorating the Exhibition, 1929, M1.21 with 'Townsend & Co.' (LAG).
5.5 Model of the Castle Keep, 1929, M1.23 (SM)
5.6 Large 23 inch plaque with hand painted group of geisha girls on a purple ground, 1929, M1.23 (GW).

45

5.6

version of the plaque with lustre and enamel painting is known but this may well have been produced for a special order.

Of the other souvenir designs the most common has an underglaze blue 'chintz' background against which are set vignettes of the Exhibition buildings, the Tyne Bridge and Newcastle's coat of arms (fig. 5.2). This design was used on a great variety of items, including some distinctly old fashioned pieces, and it appears that the firm used the opportunity of the Exhibition to use up as much of their old stock as possible. Indeed, the date stamp on some Exhibition pieces can reveal the piece to have been manufactured many years earlier, sometimes as far back as the 19th century.

A rarer Exhibition souvenir shows a view of the Exhibition buildings printed in black coupled with a photo-lithographic portrait of the Prince of Wales, later Edward VIII, who opened the Exhibition (fig. 5.4). The Prince is shown with a cigarette sticking out of his mouth – an image of royalty that would be unthinkable nowadays! Another rare souvenir is the small model of the Castle Keep at Newcastle (fig. 5.5). This is found with two marks, only one of which mentions the Exhibition.

Besides these pottery souvenirs of the Exhibition, Maling's also produced a little booklet for children called 'My Adventures with the Genii of the Teapot'. This told the story of a little girl and a quaint little man 'with a tea pot for a head' who conducted her on a tour of a pottery and showed her how a tea cup was made. The story was written for children but each page bore the rather more adult message 'Maling stands for pottery perfection since 1762'.

The photograph of Townsend's stand at the Exhibition shows that Arthur Lambert also made the most of the opportunity to show off the best that his local pottery could produce. The stand displayed two large plaques made by Maling's. One was printed and hand painted with a glamorous blue Oriental dragon on a yellow ground (plate L); the second was wholly hand painted with a group of exotic Japanese geisha girls on a purple ground (fig. 5.6). Both pieces were colourful testimonies to the high standards of decoration that the Newcastle pottery was now capable of producing.

Townsend's stand also included a display of Maling production line pieces on the theme of hunting, a theme that had probably been suggested by C.T. Maling himself who was a keen hunter and the Master of the Haydon Bridge Hunt in Northumberland. The most stylish of these hunting items was the fox's head stirrup cup (plate M); the fox's head was made with two different border prints, the border of the huntsmen illustrated and the zig-zag Tango border. Morning sets in the Huntsmen pattern were also on display.

Ringtons

Besides their own stand with Townsend's, Maling's had a further interest in the 1929 North East Coast Exhibition. This was through the stand occupied by Ringtons, a local firm of tea merchants. C.T. Maling & Sons and Ringtons were already well known to each other. There was a personal link through the friendship between the Maling family and Sam Smith, the founder of the firm and a well known figure in Newcastle society. There was also a commercial link in that since 1928 Maling's had been supplying Ringtons with pottery which the tea firm would sell to its customers via their door to door delivery vans, a familiar sight on Tyneside by the 1920s.

The first piece of pottery which Maling's had supplied to Ringtons was a square tea caddy in the blue printed Broseley pattern (illustrated MTP). This began a long association between the two firms which lasted until 1962. Ringtons sold pottery during the Christmas season and their orders were usually placed during the summer months when the London trade was slack, an added bonus for the Ford Potteries. In the 1930s Ringtons ordered batches of 15,000 pieces but by the 1950s this had increased to 40,000.

For the 1929 Exhibition, Maling's supplied Ringtons with a special range of blue printed octagonal tea caddies in four different designs. The first showed local castles, plus Windsor castle on the lid; the second showed local bridges, and the third local cathedrals. The cathedral caddy came on a tall shape to accommodate the cathedrals' tall spires but the three other versions were printed on the squat octagonal Hector shape. The fourth version was similar to the bridges caddy but had a different lid showing a view of the Exhibition buildings. The Exhibition version was sold, full of tea, at the Exhibition itself (fig. 5.7) but the others were sold over the doorsteps as usual. The price in 1929 was 6s 6d.

The association with Ringtons continued through the 1930s with two very attrac-

5.7

5.8

5.7 Ringtons' stand at the 1929 Exhibition: Maling tea caddies are prominently displayed.
5.8 Pansy flower vases made for Ringtons in the 1930s, M1.26 (LAG).

Colour Plates

E Three rosebud vases, c.1913, pn 9635 (SM).
F Page from a 1920s catalogue showing pre-1920s black ground patterns (SM).
G 1920s coloured grounds: tea caddy, M1.17; sponge dish pn 508/1, M1.17; bulb bowl, pn 318, M1.17 (DB, LAG).
H Two mid-1920s teapots: Bird border, pn 3273; Crinoline Ladies border, pn 3273, both M1.23 (LAG).
I Page from a 1920s catalogue showing mid- and late 1920s gold printed patterns (SM).
J Ginger jar and plate, early 1930s, both M1.23; fine examples of the high quality of the best lustre pieces (KW).

CE TEM WARE
REG? TRADE MARK.

9517. No. 3 Shape.

9463. No. 4 Shape.

9533. No. 1 Shape.

9480. No. 1 Shape.

9518. No. 5 Shape

Top: **F**, *Below:* **E**

G

Bon-Bon Box 3584.

Stanley Bowl (footed) 3578.

Bon-Bon Box, 3449.

County Biscuit Jar, 3072.

Beehive Inkstand, 3576.

Oval Ash Tray, 3494.

Earl Biscuit Jar, 3494.

Louis Bowl, 3581.

Chelsea Bowl, 3585.

Louis Bowl, 3586.

Top: **I**, *Below:* **H**

J

5.9

5.10

tive floral designs: the blue printed Chintz (plate N), which came on matching sets of jugs and teapots, and the moulded Pansy border (fig. 5.8). Both of these patterns still look fresh today and they are among the best known and best loved of all Maling patterns. Later in the decade Maling's began to supply Ringtons with colour lithographed pieces, such as the 'Royal Souvenir Casket' celebrating the coronation of King George VI and Queen Elizabeth in 1937, and the Homestead and Vine colour prints from the late 1930s and early 1940s (fig. 5.9).

The Ford Pottery's troubles in the aftermath of the Second World War appear to have halted the production of new designs for Ringtons but the supply resumed in 1953 when the tea firm ordered 20,000 Pekoe jugs embossed with Blossom Bough (fig. 5.10). This was followed in 1955 by an order for 44,000 Jesmond shaped tea pots embossed with Autumn Leaves, and the last order from the tea firm was in 1962 for 100,000 Grecian jugs embossed with Godetia (fig. 5.10). This last order is said to have come after Ringtons had tried out a number of samples of pottery on their customers: Godetia was the tea drinkers' choice.

The pottery made for Ringtons was usually specially designed for the tea firm and bore a special printed mark. The mark on the earliest pieces showed Ringtons' newly built head quarters in Algernon Road, Newcastle, but this later changed to Ringtons' trademark, a monogram on a shield. This mark was printed in blue on the early 1930s pieces and in green on the later ones.

5.9 Colour lithographed pieces made for Ringtons in the late 1930s, from left: 'Homestead'; the Coronation Casket, 1937; 'Vine'; M1.26 (SAG, LAG).
5.10 Two jugs made for Ringtons, from left: Blossom Bough, 1953; Godetia with its original box, 1962; both M1.26 (LAG, AB).

6.7

Chapter 6

New styles for the Jazz Age

The early 1930s saw a new character creep into Maling pottery. Patterns become simpler, brighter and more stylised; freehand painting becomes more prominent; the coloured grounds disappear giving the new patterns a fresher, lighter feel. This change of character reflected changing fashions. The late 1920s saw the large scale import from Europe of brightly coloured, hand painted pottery of, what was called at the time, the 'cottage type'. It also saw the success of the equally bright 'Bizarre' pottery produced by Wilkinson's under the name of their head designer, Clarice Cliff. Both testified to the ready market for colourful, informal pottery that reflected the fresh, new spirit of the times.

The fresh new spirit first made its appearance in Maling patterns with the zig-zag Tango border that was used on several ranges of the early 1930s, notably on the pieces commemorating the 1931 Historical Pageant of Newcastle and the North. Three different designs were produced for this occasion (fig. 6.1). The plaque painted for the occasion by Lucien Boullemier was probably not a production piece, but a 'one off' for advertising purposes (plate O).

An even more dramatic expression of the new spirit was the Anzac pattern introduced c.1931 (plate P). This not only displayed a bright new jazzy pattern but had a new angular shape, which the pottery named Jazz. Unfortunately, the Jazz shape proved to be the Anzac pattern's undoing: the tea pots dribbled and the solid handles of the cups were difficult to hold. The buyers' comments were not

6.2

6.1

6.1 Pieces commemorating the 1931 Historical Pageant of Newcastle and the North. All M1.26 (KW, SM, LAG).
6.2 Honey pot in Empress shape, 1933, pn 5882, M1.23 (SM).
6.7 Honey pot painted by Theo Maling, late 1920s, signed 'T.M.' (PC).

6.3

6.4

encouraging and the Jazz shape was eventually abandoned, with the exception of the small sugar bowls which were incorporated into more traditional coffee and morning sets. Anzac on Jazz appears to have been produced as both tea and coffee sets.

The Empress shape introduced in 1932 was more of a compromise between old and new. It was far less angularly modern than Jazz yet its wavy edged shapes with a horizontal emphasis did make some concessions to the new taste for stream-lined profiles (fig. 6.2). The simple, stylised patterns which came with it were more unambiguously up to date: as *The Pottery Gazette* noted of pattern 5742, it was 'extraordinarily simple and in strict keeping with present day demands'. As if to make up for the simplicity of the patterns, Maling's decided to add some 'emboss-ments', small patches of embossed floral sprays which were scattered around the rims of the pieces. The 'embossments' seem a rather unnecessary addition to what was basically quite a pleasing new shape, but the firm was perhaps worried that too much modern simplicity would be bad for sales.

Another gesture in the direction of modern brightness and colourfulness was the eye catching Tulip pattern (5527) with its stylised sinuous tulips (plate Q). Less ambitious, but with the same delight in colour was the cheerful floral tableware pattern (fig. 6.3), and the Butterfly pattern of 1932 (fig. 6.4). Although Butterfly gives the appearance of being wholly hand painted, as was the fashion of the time, the pattern was in fact 'smoke printed': an outline was printed in soot and oil rather than ink and after the paintresses had filled in the colours the printed outline would disappear literally in a puff of smoke when the piece was fired.

The real success story of the early 1930s for the Ford Pottery was Cobblestone kitchen ware, introduced in September 1931 and still being heavily promoted as a best selling line in January 1935. Cobblestone will be looked at in more detail in chapter 9 but it is worth mentioning here not just for its importance as the firm's best selling line of the early 1930s, a time when the Depression was at its height, but also because Cobblestone too stood for the new bright spirit of the 1930s. *The Pottery Gazette* recognised this and particularly recommended Cobblestone to dealers who dealt with the 'younger generation' who wanted their homes to be 'distinctive and modern':

> Here then is a unique chance for the progressive retailer. A special
> window show of the new Cobblestone kitchen ware, bearing the mes-
> sage: 'Don't be old fashioned; but equip your kitchen in the 1931 style'
> might be found to work wonders.

The new spirit visible in Maling patterns after 1933 could be put down to the arrival in that year of a second designer. Lucien George Boullemier (born 1898) was the son of Lucien Emile and he came to the Ford Pottery on the request of his father who saw that there was more than enough work to keep two designers fully employed. Lucien George was a useful addition. He had been brought up in the pottery business and had served his apprenticeship at Wood & Sons, under their famous Art Director Frederick Rhead; whilst at Wood's he had become great friends with Rhead's daughter Charlotte, 'Lottie', later to be famous in her own right. Apart

6.5

6.3 Morning set c. 1933, pn 5877, M1.23 (SM).
6.4 The Butterfly pattern, 1932, vase, pn 5759, M1.23; plate, pn 5645, M1.27 (SM).
6.5 Regent shape jug, 1935, Ruche Band pattern, pn 6091, M1.23 (SM). The advertisement is from *The Pottery Gazette*, February, 1935.

56

6.6

from a short spell in the forces, Boullemier had worked at Wood's all his life and had acquired experience not just of designing but also of the technological side of pottery making. This was particularly useful for the Newcastle firm.

Boullemier Jr. worked closely with his father during his initial years at the pottery (for instance, they were often to be found together 'finishing off' pieces by painting over faults that had appeared during the manufacturing process) and the first patterns that were wholly his were Pastel and Ruche Band of 1934. A more substantial contribution was the range of Regent dinner ware (fig. 6.5) which was launched in February 1935 and which was entirely, both patterns and shapes, the work of the younger man. Regent dinner ware represented a considerable step forward after the half hearted modernity of the Empress range. Gone were the fussy embossments and the floral knops, to be replaced with streamlined horizontal shapes, the high shoulders typical of the smart styles of the period, and neat wedge shaped knops and handles. The Regent shape was as uncompromisingly modern as its predecessor Jazz but it had an elegance that the aggressively chunky 1931 shape had lacked.

6.6 Theo Maling at work at the Ford Pottery, 1931 (SM).
6.8 Three ashtrays c. 1930: left, Salmon Fly, pn 3545, M1.23 with 'W.R. Pape Fishing Tackle'; flying geese, M1.23; tall trees, M1.23. The last two painted by Theo Maling and signed 'T.M.' (SM).
6.9 Vase in the Storm pattern, 1930s, M1.27 (LAG).
6.10 Maling pottery painted by amateurs probably at evening classes: no. 70 shape vase, signed 'E.H. Coney, Hand painted'; ashtray signed 'W'; small bowl signed 'Hand painted, H.C.' (SM).

6.8

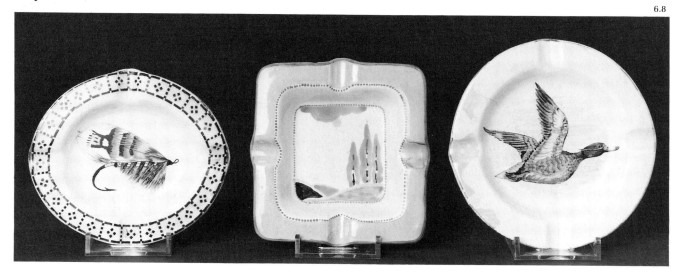

A smaller but nonetheless significant influence in the firm's new modern character was Theo Maling (fig. 6.6), Frederick Theodore Maling's daughter, who worked at the pottery for a short time in the late 1920s and early 1930s after taking the Art Diploma Course at Armstrong College, now Newcastle University. Much of Theo Maling's time at the pottery was spent painting trials and samples for Boullemier but she did experiment with patterns of her own in a variety of styles (fig. 6.7, plates S, T), some of which were adapted for production. Plate R shows Theo Maling's original freehand painted Anemone pattern and the barely distinguishable production version which is painted over an outline transfer print. Other patterns by 'Miss Theo' that were adapted for production included the Salmon Fly pattern (fig. 6.8), which was used on ashtrays made for the Newcastle fishing tackle shop W.R. Pape, the Storm pattern (fig. 6.9), and the Squiggle pattern (seen in the foreground in fig. 6.6). The last two of these were wholly freehand painted, even in their production versions, and their informal, abstract character was well in tune with the new modern spirit of the times.

The firm's freehand painted production pieces of the early 1930s should not be confused with the pieces painted in that decade by amateurs (fig. 6.10). Several of these pieces are still around and their idiosyncratic patterns often puzzle present day Maling collectors. Many of the amateur painted pieces originate from an evening class on pottery decoration taught by Theo Maling in Newcastle from c.1930 to 1936; a similar class was taught until 1931 by Peggy Bullock, daughter of the local artist Ralph Bullock, who also painted her own designs on Maling pottery (fig. 6.11). The pottery used at both these classes was Maling seconds which the firm would glaze and fire for the amateurs. One of the main ways of distinguishing these amateur pieces from the firm's own patterns is that the amateur pieces are often signed by their proud creators more elaborately than the firm would have allowed.

Another instance of Maling pottery being decorated outside the factory is provided by the Bough Pottery in Edinburgh. The Bough Pottery was a decorating concern set up in the early 1920s by Richard Amour and his family. The Amours painted their designs on to biscuit pottery (using, they promised, only freehand brushstrokes 'no transfers, air brushes, wheels or other aids are made use of in the studio'). The biscuit pottery they used was from C.T. Maling & Sons to whom

6.10

6.9

they would return the pieces after decorating for glazing and firing. The Amours claimed to sign every piece they produced so there should be no possibility of confusing their work with Maling's own pieces.

Despite all this fresh new simplicity, Maling's continued to produce their lustred and gold printed pottery; indeed, some of the firm's most lavish floral patterns come from the early 1930s. In November 1933 *The Pottery Gazette* illustrated the Peona, pn. 5508 (plate K), and Viola, pn. 5970, patterns and heaped praise on their 'highly ornate' character which 'stood out in strong contrast to many of the simpler, neater styles which are ruling in certain other quarters of the industry'. Similarly ornate were the pieces produced for the three Royal occasions that the country celebrated during the middle of the 1930s.

The first of these Royal occasions was the Silver Jubilee of King George V and Queen Mary in 1935. A range of pieces on a rich, dark blue ground was produced for this (fig. 6.12). All had a formal gold printed design of flags and national emblems surrounding the monarchs' portraits delicately finished with hand painting by the two Boullemiers. The blue ground on these pieces proved difficult to fire and although it was used for the next range of royal commemoratives, for the coronation of Edward VIII in 1937, it was later changed.

The Edward VIII pieces were more ambitious. The two designers now had the services of a good modeller (see chapter 7) and they produced a design which, although containing the same traditional elements, looked far more modern because it was embossed in shallow relief rather than printed. The design only appears to have been produced on plaques and jugs (plate U, the plaque is illustrated in MTP).

These pieces were almost certainly made as limited editions and they became

6.11

6.11 Maling plaque painted by Peggy Bullock c. 1930 and signed with her mark of a flower over the letter B (PC).

Colour Plates

K Four coffee cans and saucers, early 1930s, all M1.23. The pale lustre one is part of a set given by the Malings to the Hoults as a wedding present; the blue one is the 'Peona' pattern, pn 5508 (FH).
L Large 23 inch plaque, 'Oriental' border with additional hand colouring, 1929, M1.23 (LAG).
M Fox's head stirrup cup, 1929, M1.23 (SM).
N The Chintz pattern produced for Ringtons, c.1935. M1.26 (LAG).
O Hand painted plaque signed by Lucien Boullemier advertising Maling's Pageant Ware, 1931, M1.23 Malcolm Herdman).
P 'Anzac' pattern teaset, c.1931, M1.23 (LAG).
Q Tulip pattern vase and plate, c.1932, pn 5527, M1.23 (SM).

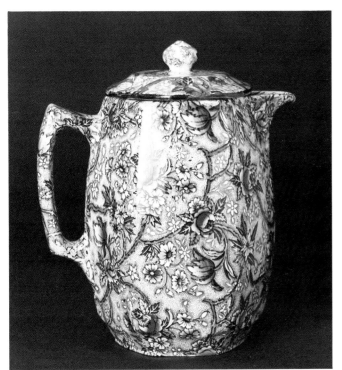

Top left: **N**, *Top right:* **M**, *Below:* **K**

L

Top: **P**, *Below:* **Q**

6.12

even rarer when most were destroyed on the announcement of the abdication, only weeks before the planned coronation. Maling's appear to have tried to salvage something from the commercial disaster of the abdication because two known examples of the Edward VIII jug bear the date of the abdication as well as that of the coronation. One of these is rather badly painted suggesting that it may have been rushed off as a trial piece to illustrate how the design might be adapted to the new circumstances. The other, however, is well finished and may have been intended for exhibition in the firm's showrooms, although it seems unlikely that anyone would have wanted to celebrate the embarrassment of the abdication. For the coronation of George VI later in 1937 the firm reverted to the old style of a gold printed formal design on a rich blue background (fig. 6.13); cheaper versions were produced with colour lithographs on a plain background.

Despite these royal projects, Lucien Emile Boullemier left the pottery late in 1936. According to his son, he felt that there was no longer sufficient work for two designers and it is also said that he wished for more recognition. The 1930s was a time when pottery designers were becoming more 'visible'; designers like Suzie Cooper and Clarice Cliff had their names printed on all their pottery whereas 'designed and modelled by Lucien Boullemier' appeared only occasionally on Maling pieces. When the Staffordshire pottery firm, the New Hall Pottery Company Ltd., offered Boullemier not only a job but also the chance to see his name on all their products, he took the opportunity and returned to Staffordshire to create the range of 'Boumier Ware' every piece of which carried his printed signature.

Despite his father's departure, Lucien George elected to stay with the Newcastle firm and through him the name of Boullemier continued to be associated with C.T. Maling & Sons until the firm's closure in 1963.

6.13

6.12 Plaque commemorating the Silver Jubilee of George V in 1935, an unusual example of this range, M1.23 (KW).
6.13 Beaker commemorating the coronation of George VI in 1937, M1.27 (KW).

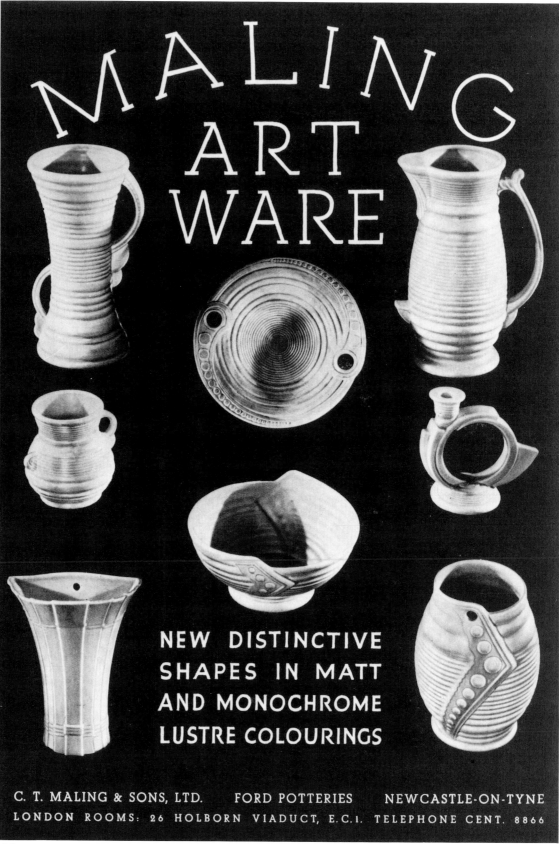

MALING ART WARE

NEW DISTINCTIVE
SHAPES IN MATT
AND MONOCHROME
LUSTRE COLOURINGS

C. T. MALING & SONS, LTD.   FORD POTTERIES   NEWCASTLE-ON-TYNE
LONDON ROOMS: 26 HOLBORN VIADUCT, E.C.1. TELEPHONE CENT. 8866

7.3

Chapter 7

The late 1930s: Maling Ware goes modern

The new spirit of modernity that had appeared at the Ford Pottery in the early 1930s, and which had been encouraged by the arrival of L.G. Boullemier in 1933, was further encouraged by the arrival in 1935 of a new modeller, Norman Carling (fig. 7.1). Carling (1902 – 1971), like many of the firm's best employees, came to Maling's from a Staffordshire firm; in his case it was A.J. Wilkinson, the firm responsible for Clarice Cliff's 'Bizarre' pottery. Carling was originally from Stockton and, according to his daughter Anne, the Malings approached him after admiring two of his Wilkinson pieces exhibited in a show in his home town.

The first Maling range by Norman Carling was Blossom Time, introduced in Autumn 1935 (fig. 7.2). This was, as *The Pottery Gazette* remarked, 'a definite remove from any decorative effect hitherto produced at Newcastle upon Tyne in the realm of fancies'. The pattern was neither printed nor embossed in outline alone, but moulded in quite heavy relief against a strongly ribbed background. A moulded design like this would not have been possible without a competent modeller. The firm had employed a modeller prior to Carling's arrival, a Mr. Bradley, but he had undertaken only very modest work. The shapes of the Blossom Time pieces displayed the typical 1930s delight in novelty and the pattern came in four up to date colour schemes: primrose yellow, pale blue, pink and green.

7.1

7.1 Norman Carling at work in 1962 with a mould for, and unglazed piece of Bambola, 1936. The photograph also shows the masks of Montgomery and Churchill he modelled for Maling's during the War (LAG, photo PC).
7.3 Matt Lustre Art Ware advertisement from *The Pottery Gazette*, July 1937.

7.2

The success of Blossom Time was followed up in Autumn 1936 by Bambola which was similar to Blossom Time in that it consisted of a cheerful heavily moulded design of flowers but this time on a background of bamboo (fig. 7.1). A second new range of 1936 was 'Matt Lustre Art Ware' (fig. 7.3, plate V) which was slightly more restrained in that it had no pictorial decoration at all but relied for its fashionable appeal on its unusual, ribbed shapes and its coloured, matt glazes. Matt colouring was an essential ingredient in 1930s pottery that had any pretensions at all to be 'artistic' and Maling decorators seem to have quickly acquired an attractive range of matt finishes. One of the most glamorous of these matt finishes was Lustreen (plate V) which mixed several matt colours on the body of the piece to produce an abstract effect that was similar in character to the earlier Storm pattern.

1938 saw a return to pictorial patterns with the introduction of Flight (plate W). Like its predecessors of the mid 1930s Flight was executed in 'matt colour schemes' on 'new artistic shapes'; the colour schemes in this case were a tasteful pale green and buff, although some pieces with more traditional underglaze glossy colours are known. Flight was different in style from Blossom Time and Bambola; its shapes were distinctly more restrained and the background ribbing was used more discreetly just around the edges of the pieces. Although it is still a design aimed at the popular market Flight has an elegance about it which the floral embossed designs lacked.

Flight seems to have been the last important range of embossed patterns that the pottery promoted before the outbreak of war but Norman Carling's hand can be seen in the production of other moulded pieces of the late 1930s: examples include the moulded floral Detia pattern of 1939; several pieces with tree trunk mouldings (plate X); a salad bowl with a lobster moulded in the base; a basket in the form of two swans. It was probably also Carling's skills that encouraged the firm to develop a more extensive range of shallow embossed patterns around the middle of the decade. Embossed plaques seem to have been particularly successful (fig. 7.4) and were still being made in large quantities during the 1940s and 1950s. Many of the designs on these embossed plaques were adapted from earlier printed

7.2 Blossom Time shapes (LAG).
7.4 Three embossed plaques, late 1930s-1940s: Cottage Garden; Tulip, pn 6451; Galleon, pn 6314. All M1.27 (SM, LAG).
7.5 Figure group, 1938, hand painted mark 'Malings 1938' (SM).
7.6 Bust of Anne Carling aged 6, modelled by her father in 1944 (PC).

7.4

7.5

7.6

patterns; the Galleon pattern, for instance, had first made its appearance in the mid 1920s.

Perhaps the two most impressive examples of Norman Carling's skills are the two large vases which he modelled in the mid 1940s: the Perseus and Andromeda vase, and the Sea-gulls vase. The Perseus and Andromeda vase (illustrated TP) was made in 1946 and it depicted the mythological tale of Perseus saving Andromeda from a dragon. Only three of these vases were produced although a fourth is said to have been spoilt in the kiln and abandoned. The circumstances surrounding the production of the Sea-gulls vase (plate Y) are not known but it was probably also made in the mid 1940s. At this time the pottery was still in the difficult aftermath of the Second World War and both vases must have provided the firm's directors with a frustrating reminder of the high quality work that the Ford Pottery could still produce.

Carling also seems to have been frustrated by the aftermath of the war. In 1946 he left the pottery with the Ford Pottery's engraver, Cecil Parker, to set themselves up in business making figures and other ornaments in plaster. However, Norman Carling continued to work for several pottery firms, including Maling's, on a free-lance basis and many of the shapes used in the 1950s Maling ranges were from his hand.

One important consequence of Norman Carling's arrival in 1935 was that for the first time Maling's began to consider the production of figures. Their new modeller was quite capable of modelling three dimensional designs, as the bust of his daughter Anne (fig. 7.6) shows. Unfortunately, although several trial samples were produced, none went into full production. The reason for this, according to Lucien George Boullemier, was the failure of the buyers to place any orders, and this in turn was explained by the domination of the figure market by a few well established firms, notably Royal Doulton.

A few Maling trial figures do, nevertheless, survive, and they give us some idea of the range that was being offered to the buyers during the late 1930s and early 1940s. One of the figures that seems to survive in relatively large numbers is Lady Nicotine, a dainty crinolened lady who conceals under her bright green or yellow lustre skirts three ashtrays and a cigarette holder. More robust in style was a group

7.8

7.7

7.9

of typically 1930s chubby-cheeked children perching on a rustic log (fig. 7.5). One of the surviving examples of this group bears a hand painted date, 1938. Equally 'of the period' is a reclining woman (fig. 7.9), and 'Snip' the Scottie dog (fig. 7.8) who was modelled from life from the dog that belonged to Mrs. Graham, Mr. C.T. Maling's housekeeper. Norman Carling seems to have been particularly fond of elephants and two Maling model elephants have been recorded (fig. 7.7). A list of moulds used at the pottery suggests that many other samples were produced, among them a Scottish Highlander, an Old Boot, even garden ornaments such as tortoises, owls and rabbits. The trial of figures was not a success and it seems likely that with the departure of Norman Carling in 1946, even the trials were abandoned.

With the new emphasis in the second half of the 1930s on novel moulded shapes, it is quite surprising to find the printed patterns reverting to more traditional, even old fashioned, designs. Lucien George Boullemier continued to follow his father's practice of producing good quality and traditional looking floral patterns set against a coloured, often lustred, background (figs. 7.11, 7.12). Anemone, heavily prom-

7.10

7.13

7.7 Elephant, modelled by Norman Carling, late 1930s (SM).
7.8 Snip, modelled by Norman Carling, late 1930s (LAG).
7.9 Seated woman, modelled by Norman Carling, late 1930s (PC).
7.10 Bowl, Anemone pattern, pn 6384, c. 1937, M1.23 (LAG).
7.11 Vase, Starflower pattern, late 1930s, M1.23 (LAG).
7.12 Three late 1930s lustre patterns: pair of Bristol shape vases pn 6322; no 6 vase in 'Rosine' pattern, pn 6470; all M1.23 (KW, DB).
7.13 Late 1930s floral patterns: plaque, Primrose, pn 6404; bowl, Garland, pn 6450; dessert bowl, May Bloom, pn 6481; all M1.23 (LAG).
7.14 Two tulip candlesticks, late 1930s, M1.27 (Dr. and Mrs. C. Bell).

7.11

7.12

7.14

oted in 1938, was typical with its luscious large flowers and glamorous gold print-ing (fig. 7.10). The following year the pottery made a special feature of its lustre bowls, 'the ideal gift', all of which would not have looked out of place in an advertisement of 1929. Waved backgrounds continued to be used liberally on unlustred pieces; good examples are the late 1930s patterns in figure 7.13. These floral patterns proved continuously popular and the pottery continued to produce them throughout the 1940s and in some cases well into the 1950s as well.

Boullemier also continued the time-honoured pottery practice of reworking older prints to suit the changing taste of the market. The 1939 advertisement for a new range of ornamental ware, Briar Rose, calls it 'a new design by Maling's' but the print was already over 40 years old and had originally been called not Briar Rose but Osborne. What was new about the design was the new elongated and undulating shapes by Norman Carling, and also the fashionably pastel background colours: powder blue, powder green, and powder rose.

Besides these floral patterns which were all coloured in by hand, the pottery used some rather unadventurous colour lithographs on its tableware of the late 1930s. By this time the pottery was buying in lithographs from outside suppliers and lithographs tended to be used on the cheaper goods made in large quantities: the ordinary souvenir beakers produced for the coronation of George VI in 1937 are good examples.

8.7

Chapter 8

The 1950s: Maling Lustre Ware

The decorative pottery produced by Maling's during the 1950s and early 1960s was, as *The Pottery Gazette* remarked in 1952, 'distinctive and not easily confused with the products of North Staffordshire'. 1950s Maling is also not easily confused with the products of the Ford Pottery during the 1920s and 1930s. The 1950s colours tended to be brighter and more metallic; the pieces were more thickly potted; and the clay body was whiter and more 'mass produced' in its general appearance, largely because Maling's no longer mixed their own bodies but brought in standard batches of clay 'mix' from suppliers in Staffordshire.

Maling pottery from the 1950s is in some ways less interesting to the collector than the earlier pieces for the simple reason that far fewer patterns were made: between 1950 and 1960 an average of 11 designs a year were introduced, compared with an average of 240 a year between 1920 and 1930. Furthermore, those designs that were produced tended to have a similar character: all were lustred, used a similar palette of colours, and tended to be rather 'safe'. During the 1950s Maling's advertised their decorative pottery as 'beautiful creations with universal appeal' and this sums up the glamorous yet conservative character of Maling pottery during its final years.

A new sequence of printed patterns was begun in 1950 and in 1952 five were singled out for mention by *The Pottery Gazette* as being particularly popular: Springtime, Garland, Chintz, Rosalind and Venetian Scenes. The best known of these is probably Springtime which was advertised as a 'design of charm and colour' on its introduction in 1950. Springtime was a simple border print of spring

8.1

8.1 1950s floral patterns: ginger jar, 'Peony Rose' pn 6569; bowl 'Rosalind', pn 6546; candlestick 'Springtime', pn 6524; all M1.23 (LAG).
8.7 Voluta ewer and flower holder c.1960, all M1.25 (LAG).

8.2

8.3

flowers set against a coloured waved background. Although it was a new design its general character owed a lot to the earlier floral patterns produced in the 1930s. Garland was in fact a straight revival of a 1930s pattern and both Rosalind, introduced in 1952 as a 'harmonious blend of colour and the potter's art', and Peony Rose, 1953, had a similar character, although the 1950s floral prints tend to have more 'space' in them than the busy 1930s prints (fig. 8.1). These floral prints were used extensively and many pieces with these patterns are still in circulation. Some of the later floral patterns, Dahlia, Golden Spray and Brocade (fig. 8.2), were also traditional looking but were given a slightly more modern aspect by being printed on modern shapes against new matt or pastel lustre backgrounds.

Not all of the printed patterns were floral. Two of the patterns mentioned by *The Pottery Gazette* in 1952, Venetian Scenes and Chintz, offered a variation in style and both made use of the Ford Pottery's stock of old copper printing plates. Chintz was a brown version of the pretty print that had been used for Ringtons pieces in the 1930s. Venetian Scenes (fig. 8.3) used a print that had last been seen in the 1920s but which looks as if it dated back to the 19th century. The 1950s version of Venetian Scenes is usually printed in brown, although it is sometimes seen in green, pink and purple, and it is surrounded by a larger vine border than that used on the 1920s version. Both prints were further updated by being covered with the ubiquitous lustre glaze.

Another example of the revival of an earlier print was the series of Poor Richard's Way to Wealth prints which had last been seen in Robert Maling's time. The prints were applied to mugs (fig. 8.4) which were regularly ordered by a transatlantic shipping company as souvenirs for their passengers; some Poor Richard mugs bear the shipping company's insignia on the reverse. Apparently, the mugs also did very well in the American market and were ordered in large quantities by Maling's American agents, the Cornforth China Company. The Poor Richard pieces were produced as a series from 1952 onwards.

Many embossed patterns of the 1950s drew heavily on 1930s designs either by using the same basic pattern but applying it to a more up to date shape, or by altering the colour and treatment of the design to suit the 1950s market. Bambola and Blossom Time were both re-issued in the 1950s and the 1950s versions are recognisable by the lustrous mother of pearl colouring. Blossom Time's basic design was also adapted to a new embossed pattern, Cherry Blossom (fig. 8.9), whose shapes were a little more up to date.

Like the printed patterns, the most popular embossed patterns appear to have been the traditional looking floral ones such as Godetia of 1952 (fig. 8.5), 'a design

73

8.5

8.2 No. 55 shape vase 'Brocade' 1958; Luxor tray 'Dahlia' 1960, M1.23 (AB, LAG).
8.3 Venetian Scenes vase, 1950, pn 6532, M1.23 (SAG).
8.4 Five Poor Richard mugs, 1952-1962, all M1.23 (KW).
8.5 Godetia cake plate, 1953, pn 6552, M1.23 (SAG).
8.6 Shapes from a 1960s pattern card: top 'Rosemarie and Harlequin Shapes'; bottom 'Floret' (LAG).
8.8 Shapes from a 1960s pattern card including Pewter Rose and Voluta (LAG).

8.4

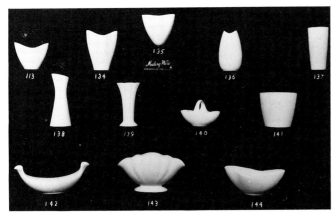

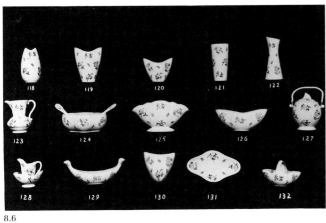

8.6

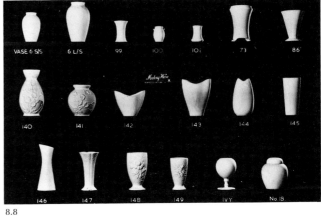

8.8

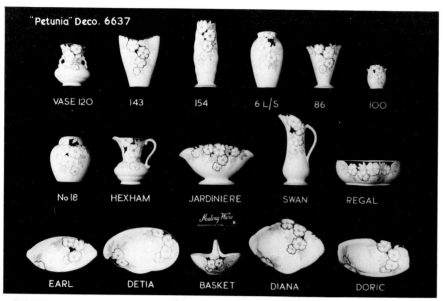

"Petunia" Deco. 6637

VASE 120   143   154   6 L/S   86   100

No 18   HEXHAM   JARDINIÉRE   SWAN   REGAL

EARL   DETIA   BASKET   DIANA   DORIC

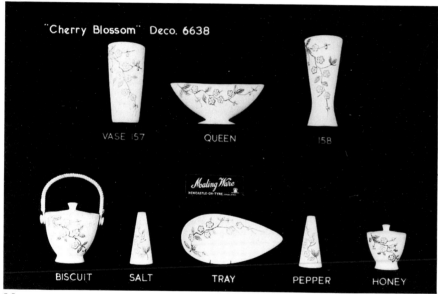

"Cherry Blossom" Deco. 6638

VASE 157   QUEEN   158

BISCUIT   SALT   TRAY   PEPPER   HONEY

8.9

of classical shape and colourful design'. Slightly more adventurous were the two patterns introduced in the early 1960s, Cameo and Floret (fig. 8.6), both of which set tasteful little white sprigs against a matt background of artistic colours such as Wedgwood blue or sage green. Shallow border embossments were also revived in the 1950s, notably on the limited edition plaques hand painted by Lucien George Boullemier for the coronation of Elizabeth II in 1953 (fig. 8.11).

Maling's 1950s shapes seem to be slightly more adventurous than their patterns. Several distinctively 1950s shapes made their appearance towards the end of the decade, among them Voluta (figs. 8.7, 8.8), a rather glamorous concoction of elliptical curves that could look almost overpowering when drenched with a vividly coloured lustre glaze. Other 1950s elliptical shapes included the Gondola Boat, the Luxor tray, and that peculiarly 1950s invention, the T.V. cup and saucer.

Several new asymmetric shapes were made for the Harlequin pattern (fig. 8.6), a typically 1950s abstract lozenge design, and these were also used for a revival of Storm; the 1950s version of Storm has stronger blue colours than its 1930s predecessor. The modern Harlequin shapes were also used for the Two Tone pat-

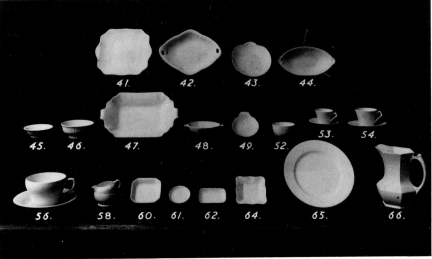

8.10

8.11

tern of the early 1960s which consisted of two coloured matt glazes merging into each other.

The pattern cards reproduced in this chapter illustrate most of the shapes that were still in use at the time of the Ford Pottery's closure in 1963. Unsurprisingly, they show a mixture of old and new: old 19th century teapots next to new elliptical vases. This combination of old and new was typical of C.T. Maling & Sons' last decade and probably says more about the firm's financial insecurity rather than the abilities of the designers and decorators. The large scale introduction of up to date designs involved a commercial risk that the firm in the 1950s just could not afford to take.

8.9 Shapes from a 1960s pattern card: 'Petunia', 1961, and 'Cherry Blossom', 1962 (LAG).
8.10 Shapes from a 1960s pattern card (LAG).
8.11 Coronation plaque, hand painted by L.G. Boullemier, 1953 (photograph courtesy Tony Boullemier).

MAIGNEN'S PATENT "FILTRE RAPIDE"
BIJOU Nº 1P

9.2

Chapter 9

Jam jars, jelly moulds and just about everything else

Jam jars and food containers

It is easy to forget that the foundation of the Malings' success was not glamorous decorative pottery but the humble jam jar. Although C.T. Maling & Sons were not the only company to make earthenware jars, they were almost certainly the largest producers. A description of the Ford B Pottery published in 1894 underlines the scale of production:

> On the occasion of our visit we were shown a stack of preserve jars
> thirty yards long by sixteen yards wide and eighteen jars deep, which
> at a rough computation must have contained over a million jars, all
> made to the standard, and for the use of a well known firm of jam man-
> ufacturers.

This well known firm was almost certainly Keiller's, whose custom lasted from the middle of the 19th century until the 1930s. Several sizes of jars were produced from the massive 2lb jar to a miniature version, one of which was used to furnish the kitchen in Queen Mary's famous dolls house. Other firms who used Maling jam jars (fig. 9.1) included Frank Cooper's, Lipton's, Sainsbury's, and John Moir & Sons of Aberdeen whose screw top jars were a registered design, not apparently registered in C.T. Maling's name.

Maling's also produced jars for other sorts of foodstuffs, such as anchovy paste, and pharmaceutical preparations. Most of these jars were decorated with a simple

9.1

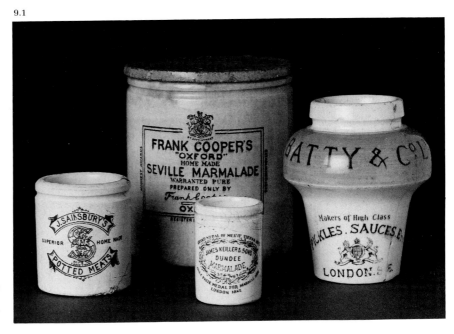

9.1 Commercial jam jars, late 19th century, M1.10 and M1.12 (SM, LAG).
9.2 Water filter, made for P.A. Maignen, 1880s, M1.12 (LAG).

black transfer print naming the retailer. The trade in all these packaging jars suffered with the expansion of the glass container industry in the early years of the 20th century although Maling's continued to supply jam jars to Keiller's and Frank Cooper's until the 1930s.

C.C. goods

'C.C. ware' was the term used to describe basic, functional undecorated pottery made in a cream or white body. The opening of the Ford B Pottery in 1879 enabled Maling's to introduce a vast range of these C.C. goods, from toilet basins and surgical dishes, to water filters and pudding basins. Most C.C. items were left plain but decoration could be applied if the customer wished (fig. 9.2).

Hospitals, hotels and other institutions were good customers for C.C. goods, and the Ford Pottery's customers included every type of institution from the Newcastle Breweries, who ordered ash trays for their pubs (fig. 9.4), to the Grand Hotel in Bullawayo. Maling pottery also found its way abroad through the shipping lines which Maling's began to supply with goods in the early years of the century: customers included the Furness line and the Albion Steamship Company. Another important customer for C.C. goods was the Government who ordered plain crockery in large quantities for use in forces canteens.

One section of the C.C. trade was the supply of standard measure mugs and jugs. These items had to be checked by the local Weights and Measures Office to ensure that the capacities were correct, and as the Ford Pottery was said to produce over 100,000 of these standard measures a year, a Weights and Measures officer was stationed permanently at the pottery. The finished goods were stamped with the official stamp, consisting of the initials of the monarch (VR, ER, GR etc.) above '71' the Newcastle district's number, and sometimes the last two digits of the year of manufacture. Standard measures were often left undecorated, but they could be decorated cheaply with coloured bands or the seaweed 'mocha' decoration (fig. 9.5).

If institutional customers required decorated pottery, Maling's could of course supply it, either printed with simple one colour transfer prints, such as the ever popular willow pattern, or decorated with colour lithographs. Good examples of the smarter end of the C.C. market are the colour lithographed pieces supplied to Newcastle's famous tea rooms 'Tilley's' (fig. 9.6). Interestingly, Tilley's cups and saucers are made out of porcelain, rather than pottery; many Maling tea services

9.3

9.3 Crockery made for various companies in the 1920s (SM).

Colour Plates

R The Anenome pattern: right, painted by Theo Maling, signed 'T.M.'; left, the outline printed production piece, c.1932, pn 5803, M1.23 (SM).
S Fish vase painted by Theo Maling, 1931, signed 'T. Maling, hand painted, Maling Ware' (PC).
T Tall trees plate painted by Theo Maling, 1933 (SM).
U An unglazed example and two glazed versions of the jug designed for the coronation of Edward VIII in 1936 (SM, KW).
V Matt Art Ware pieces, 1936, pns 6344, 6375, M1.27 (SM, LAG).
W Flight jug and bowl, 1938, M1.27 (SM).
X Tree trunk teapots and vase, late 1930s, M1.27 (AB, SM, KW).
Z Cobblestone kitchen ware, early 1930s (DB, LAG, Ian Sharp).

S

Top: **R**, *Below left:* **T**, *Below right:* **U**

Top: **V**, *Below:* **W**

Top: **X**, *Below:* **Z**

9.4

9.6

9.5

9.4 Newcastle Breweries ashtrays, 1928; ashtray for Sunderland's Seaburn Hotel c.1930; 'Abbey Cider' mug, c.1960. All M1.23 (LAG, KW).
9.5 Mocha ware measure mugs and jugs from the 1890s (LAG).
9.6 Crockery for Newcastle restaurants: teacup and saucer for Tilley's; coffee can for Rinaldo's cream jug for Lockhart's (LAG).

from this period have china cups and saucers because this was what the customer required. The china cups were bought 'in the white' from Staffordshire firms and decorated at the Ford Pottery.

Kitchen ware, and other domestic goods

Maling's did not just produce C.C. goods for institutions. From the 1880s onwards they made a large range of domestic ware, from jelly moulds to dog troughs; from invalid feeders to photographic equipment for the amateur photographer. The pages from the 1920s catalogue show the wide range of plain white domestic goods that the firm produced (figs. 9.8 – 9.11). During the late nineteenth century kitchen goods tended to be left white since they were only intended for 'below stairs'. By the 1920s, by which time the number of households with servants was declining, kitchen ware began to be decorated to appeal to the householder. Maling's range of Evergreen kitchen ware was decorated with a simple green band.

Cobblestone of 1931 (fig. 9.7, plate Z) was even more decorative and was aimed fair and square at the householder who wanted to make their kitchen a 'cheerful room of the household'. Cobblestone was enormously successful. It was originally made only in brown but by 1932 it was being produced in blue and green. The print was applied to a full range of kitchen utensils from bowls and storage jars to dredgers and rolling pins. Cobblestone continued to be produced throughout the 1930s. The exact date when the range was dropped is not known but there is no evidence that Cobblestone was produced after the Second World War.

As the Ford Pottery's trade in jam jars was hit by the expansion of the glass container industry, so the kitchen ware trade was hit by the expansion of the plastics industry after the Second World War. Nevertheless C.C.canteen goods continued to play an important part in the pottery's life right up to the end. Indeed, as has been mentioned in chapter one, it was the loss of the contract to supply crockery to the North Eastern Railway, that precipitated the pottery's closure in 1963.

9.7

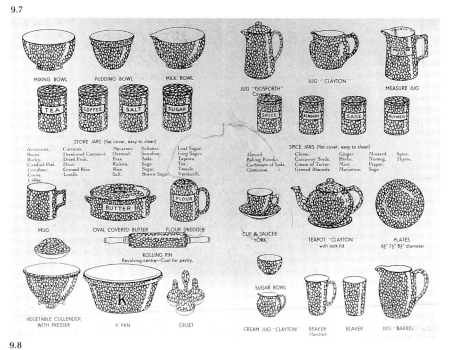

9.8

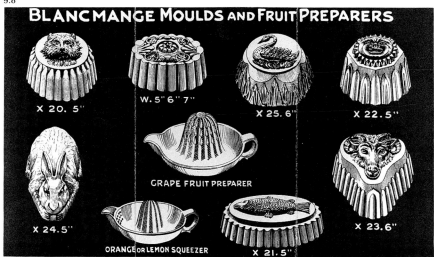

9.9

9.11

9.10

9.12

9.7 Cobblestone sales leaflet, early 1930s (SM).
9.8 Maling jelly moulds, 1930s leaflet (SM).
9.9-9.11 Pages of white ware from a late 1920s catalogue (SM).
9.12 Clay pigeon made for Pape's; plaque made for The Society of Antiquaries of Newcastle upon Tyne from a Romano British mould, 1928 (SM, LAG).

Miscellaneous pottery

Some Maling pottery does not fit into any of the usual categories, and it is perhaps fitting to end this book with two of these more unusual pieces, if only to underline what a wide range of goods the firm produced. C.T. Maling & Sons were never averse to 'having a go' and if it could be made out of clay they would try it. The first piece is a small cast produced for the Society of Antiquaries of Newcastle upon Tyne in the 1920s from a late 2nd century mould excavated at Corbridge, a fort on Hadrian's Wall. The mould was originally intended for terracotta plaques and it is said to depict the Celtic equivalent of the Roman God, Jupiter; one of these casts is now in the Museum of Antiquities in Newcastle. Collectors should not confuse these Maling casts with similar casts made not from pottery but from plaster.

The second piece is a clay pigeon made for the Newcastle gun maker W.R. Pape. These clay pigeons must have been produced in large quantities but now, of course, they are extremely rare. The example illustrated only escaped being shot to pieces by being taken home by a member of the Maling family for use as a feeding bowl for a pet rabbit. Both of these unusual pieces are illustrated in figure 9.12.

Appendix 1: Maling marks

With the exception of the very early pieces, Maling pottery is usually well marked. Besides the basic factory mark (*section 1* in this list), Maling pottery can bear impressed year numbers (*section 2*), pattern names (*section 3*), decorators' marks (*section 4*), impressed shape numbers (*section 5*), or pattern numbers (*section 6*). All of these marks can help in dating a piece of Maling but bear in mind that all of the marks must be taken account of. For instance, a piece might have a 1920s pattern number but an impressed year mark for 1940: this would indicate that the piece is a 1940s piece decorated with an older pattern. Alternatively, a piece might have an impressed year mark for 1929 but be decorated with a latter pattern: this would indicate that the pottery was using up some of the old undecorated stock that was sometimes allowed to accumulate in the warehouse.

Section 1: Basic factory marks

Marks are printed unless otherwise stated.

Pre-1853 marks

1.1 (impressed)   1.2   1.3

    MALING

1.1 is found on obviously early pieces, including 2 creamware plates dated 1828. Variants include a star above the name, and a rope border. A variant of 1.2 has the words 'semi china' in a straight line. Care should be taken with mark 1.3 which is only 6mm. long; in the 1880s the firm used a similar but larger mark, see 1.13 below.

1.4 (impressed)   1.5   1.6

   **RM**

These three marks all appear on pieces which seem to date from the 1830s or 1840s. Robert Maling may have adopted his full name when his brother John moved to the Old Ouseburn Pottery in the mid-1830s.

1853-1908

1.7 (impressed)   1.8   1.9

C.T. MALING

Probably only used in the 1850s and 1860s. 1.9 is very similar to a Davenport mark.

1.10 (impressed, various sizes)

This is the mark impressed on the underneath of Maling's jam-jars. A similar mark has the average capacity of the jar (e.g. 'Average 1lb' or 'Average 2lb') instead of the word 'Newcastle'. This mark is often found with an impressed 'K' which is supposed to stand for Keiller's, but which is certainly found on jars made for other jam firms.

1.11   1.12 (impressed)

This triangle mark was Maling's major mark from the opening of the Ford B pottery until 1908 and it was registered as a trademark in June, 1886 (number 53,801). There is a possibility that it was being used prior to that date but according to Maling's entry in the 1886 Trademarks Journal, the mark was not in use before 1875.

1.13   1.14   1.15

MALING

Probably from the 1880s and 1890s. Variants include the addition of 'England'.

1.16

The mark used on imported porcelain to cover up the original maker's mark underneath.

Cetem ware marks, 1908-1930s

1.17   1.18 (impressed)

Both marks were registered in 1908 and were the pottery's major factory marks until 1924. The printed Cetem Ware mark continued to be used until the 1930s at least but the impressed mark only seems to occur on pre-1920 pieces. The Cetem Ware sunburst can be printed in any colour ink, including gold,

---

and there are a number of small variations in the appearance of the castle and the sunburst which is sometimes found without rays.

1.19   1.20

Mark 1.19 is found on 1920s and 1930s pieces, not necessarily cheaper ones. Mark 1.20 is a rather mysterious mark that only appears on pieces of the late 1920s. Although 'Coronet' claims to be a registered trade mark, it does not appear to have been registered in Great Britain.

Maling castle marks, 1924-1963

1.21   M1.22   M1.23

The standard Maling marks from 1924 until the pottery's end in 1963. These marks can be printed in any colour ink and there are many variations in the castle and the wording around it.

1.24   1.25

Mark 1.24 was introduced by Hoults in 1947. Mark 1.25 is the rubber stamped mark used in the late 1950s and 1960s. It is noticeably cruder than the earlier transfer printed versions and sometimes has 'Estd. 1762' around the rim.

Other Maling marks

1.26   1.27

MalingWare

Both from the 1930s. Mark 1.26 is found on the 1931 Historical Pageant pieces and beneath the Ringtons' trade mark on Ringtons' pieces. Mark 1.27 is found on the 1936 coronation pieces and several of the late 1930s moulded patterns.

Some Maling figures have a hand painted mark, 'Maling England'. Pieces produced for the forces have a special printed mark with Maling's name and a royal monogram. Pieces made for the R.A.F. are marked 'R.A.F. Maling', often with the year of manufacture, such as '1942'.

Section 2: Impressed year marks

From the 1880s until the 1940s Maling's impressed many of their pieces with the year of manufacture. These numbers are usually small and give both the month and the year of manufacture. Thus '9.02' is September 1902; '12.33' is December 1933.

Before the 1920s these impressed year marks were combined with one of two letter codes to indicate the type of ceramic body being used: 'C.C' is the ordinary cream coloured body; 'S.S' is superior semi-porcelain. These letters are usually impressed just above the year numbers.

Section 3: Pattern names and registered designs

In common with most potteries Maling's often included pattern names in their marks. In the 19th century some patterns were given their own special printed mark, which usually displayed the name of the pattern in a scroll, cartouche, or vignette. Examples include: Japan, Ford, Wild Flowers, Asiatic Pheasants, Concordia and Denon's Egypt. Most of these pattern marks are easily recognisable as Maling marks because they include Maling's name, the initials CTM, or the words 'Ford Pottery'.

The use of specially printed marks seems to have died out by 1900 and thereafter Maling's pattern names were just printed beneath the basic factory mark. Examples include 'Eversley' beneath the triangle mark; 'Old Hylton' beneath the Cetem Ware mark, 'Anzac' beneath the Maling castle mark. If the pattern was a registered design, the registration number was also printed.

Registered patterns

Maling's took out 108 patents of design between 1886 and 1930. Many were for shapes. The following is a selective list of the more common registered printed patterns.

Number	Year	Pattern name
107747	1888	Kilda
107887	1888	Unnamed geometric border print
213170	1893	York
213488	1893	Jesmond
236585	1894	Arcadia
282777	1896	Portland
519756	1908	Chelsea
519757	1908	Empire
519758	1908	Lesbury
520677	1908	Florence
525716	1908	Lithograph laurel leaf border
525717	1908	Unnamed border print of small circles
589510	1911	Maltese
613498	1913	Oban
632985	1914	Duchess
745864-5	1929	Bridge tea caddies

Section 4: Decorators' marks

The pottery paintresses were required to mark their pieces with a small hand painted mark to identify their work. Most chose a letter or their initials, thus 'T' is Janet Taylor's mark. These decorators' marks are found on most pieces from the 1920s and 1930s.

Section 6: Pattern numbers

Pattern numbers were usually hand painted on to the piece by the decorators. Maling's appear to have used two main sequences of pattern numbers: the first probably running from c.1883 to c.1918, and the second running from c.1908 to the end of the pottery's life. A partial list of the patterns in this last sequence is printed in MTP. Although this list is reliable in its matching of pattern numbers to names, the dates for the pre-1952 patterns are less sure. The present list gives what we hope is a more accurate skeleton of the two main pattern number sequences.

Pattern number	Date range	Example
1 – 8000	c.1883 – 1908	150 Ivy Leaves, c.1885
8000 – 9000 } 1000 – 2000 }	1908 – 1912	8560 mentioned in 1910 8639 Poona, 1910
9000 – 9999 } 2000 – 2600 }	1912 – 1920	2428 mentioned in 1913 99989 mentioned in 1918 2694 mentioned in 1920
2600 – 3000	1920 – 1926	2856 Milan, 1924 2889 Plum and Orchard, 1926 3040 mentioned in 1927
3000 – 3500	1926 – 1929	3198 Satsuma Dragon, 1926 3273 Bird border, 1926
3500 – 4000	1929 – 1930	3930 Old Mill, 1930
4000 – 5500	1930 – 1932	5259 Storm, 1931 5488 Anzac, 1931 5595 mentioned in 1932
5500 – 6000	1932 – 1934	5855 Peona, 1933 5971 mentioned in 1933
6000 – 6500	1934 – 1940s	6237 Blossom Time, 1935 6357 Bambola, 1936 6384 Anemone, 1937 6423 Flight, 1938 6442 Briar Rose, 1939 6450 Garland, 1940
6524 – 6570	1950 – 1955	6524 Springtime, 1950 6561 Peony Rose, 1953
6570 – 6610	1955 – 1960	6586 Brocade, 1958 6604 Harlequin, 1959
6610 – 6639	1960 – 1963	6610 Floret, 1960 6619 Two tone, 1962

Section 5: Impressed mould numbers

Some Maling pieces bear impressed numbers, 1 cm high, much larger than the small year numbers. These are shape or mould numbers: Two of the most common are:
3054 on beakers
2085 on beakers
Many of the new shapes introduced by Norman Carling in the mid 1930s bear single or two digit impressed numbers.

A note on sources

The main published source for the pottery's history in the 20th century is *The Pottery Gazette and Glass Trades Review* which contains many small references to C.T. Maling & Sons in the monthly *Buyer's Notes* sections. Articles on the whole pottery are found in the June 1916 and June 1952 issues.

The most useful of the other published sources have been:

C.T. Maling, "On the Manufacture of Earthenware", in *The Industrial Resources of the Tyne, Wear and Tees*, ed. W.G. Armstrong and others (1864) pp. 205-206. This article is also included in *A History of the Trade and Manufacturers of the Tyne, Wear and Tees*, ed. R. Welford (1863) pp. 183-4. The information was incorporated into Llewellyn Jewitt's *The Ceramic Art of Great Britain* (1878) which contains some additional descriptions of local potteries.

Heath, H. and Maling, C.T., "The Manufacture of Earthenware", in *Handbook to the Industries of Newcastle*, ed. Wigham Richardson (1889) pp. 189-192.

A descriptive account of Newcastle (1894) pp. 65-66.

Tyneside Industries (1889) p. 101 (reproduced in MTP)

Newcastle and Tyneside, contemporary sketches and reviews (c.1903) p.101.

The Monthly Journal of the Newcastle and Gateshead Incorporated Chamber of Commerce (August 1927), p. 82.

The Institution of Electrical Engineers, Summer Meeting Handbook (1929) pp. 76-80.

Sally Madge, "The Maling Factory and Workers", *Clay, Journal of the Northern Potters Association*, no. 13 (1981).

M.A.V. Gill "The potteries of the Tyne and Wear and their dealings with the Beilby Bewick Workshop", *Archaeologia Aeliana*, 5th series, vol. IV (1976) pp. 151-170.

Information about the Maling family comes from the Corder Mss. in Sunderland Local History Library, and the Hodgson family trees (vol. 1 p. 247 and vol. V pp. 142-145) in Newcastle Local History Library. Some of this family information appears in two articles in *Antiquities of Sunderland*, vol. VII (1906).